Movements of
Educational Reform

Movements of Educational Reform

A Short Introduction Under The Lens of Change
—From the Early 1960s to the Early 2000s

DAVID A. ESCOBAR ARCAY

RESOURCE *Publications* • Eugene, Oregon

MOVEMENTS OF EDUCATIONAL REFORM
A Short Introduction Under The Lens of Change—From the Early 1960s to the Early 2000s

Copyright © 2016 David A. Escobar Arcay. All rights reserved. Except for brief quotations in critical publications or reviews, no part of this book may be reproduced in any manner without prior written permission from the publisher. Write: Permissions, Wipf and Stock Publishers, 199 W. 8th Ave., Suite 3, Eugene, OR 97401.

Resource Publications
An Imprint of Wipf and Stock Publishers
199 W. 8th Ave., Suite 3
Eugene, OR 97401

www.wipfandstock.com

PAPERBACK ISBN: 978-1-4982-9108-8
HARDCOVER ISBN: 978-1-4982-9110-1
EBOOK ISBN: 978-1-4982-9109-5

Manufactured in the U.S.A.   09/22/16

Contents

Introduction | vii

1 The Innovation and Diffusion Period | 1
2 School Effectiveness and School Improvement | 14
3 Restructuring and Reculturing | 34
4 Large Scale Reforms | 57

Bibliography for Innovation and Diffusion Period | 87
Bibliography for School Effectiveness and School Improvement | 91
Bibliography for School Restructuring and Reculturing | 95
Bibliography for Large Scale Reforms | 99

Introduction

Multiple and diverse efforts to change and better public schools have taken place since the 1960s. This book attempts to describe various movements of educational reform that cover since the early 1960s to the early 2000s. It identifies, describes, and analyzes four movements: innovation and diffusion, school effectiveness and school improvement, school restructuring and reculturing, and large-scale reforms. These movements often if not always overlap each other. As the history of the past forty-five years unfolds, it does so not in clearly delineated straight line yearly segments, but more in a disjointed, canonical fashion. Through citing major studies, origins, and major proponents, philosophical underpinnings and practical implications for reform and theory are addressed. This book aims not only to present these four movements of educational reform but also evaluate them in terms of their potential for educational change. In order to accomplish this objective, at the end of each chapter, I will present a brief comment on the contributions of noted scholar on educational change Michael Fullan towards that particular educational reform movement.

1

The Innovation and Diffusion Period

Since the early 1960s, efforts to improve public schools have generated various approaches to bringing about educational change. Two of these approaches concern school restructuring and reculturing. This chapter examines the legacy of these two vehicles of school improvement. It first outlines the antecedents of school restructuring. Then it explores the origins, meanings, and strategies of school restructuring as well as key studies. The following chapter explicates school reculturing by investigating the origins and types of culture, describing the advocates, meanings ,and models of school culture as well as several of its key theoretical and empirical analyses and studies. Finally, Fullan's assessment of school restructuring and reculturing is explored in order to capture his contribution within this period.

During the late 1950s, the Soviet Union successfully launched the world's first artificial satellite to orbit the earth. This launch ushered in numerous technological, military, scientific, and political developments. One of the reactions in the United States was that the American education system "was not producing enough scientists and perhaps more important, that its teaching techniques and curricula were effectively extinguishing students' interest in science and scientific careers."[1] Thus, the United States' federal government initiated a number of large scale innovations and curriculum projects especially in math and science.[2] Among the curriculum reform projects were the Physical Sciences Study Committee highschool physics curriculum, the Biological Sciences Curriculum Study and Man: A Course of Study. Most of these curriculum designs were intended to accomplish and deliver content organized around key concepts that revealed the structure of the disciplines of physics and biology in addition to pedagogical methodologies. These were accompanied by reform initiatives in the organization of teaching that included flexible scheduling, team teaching, and open plan schools. These major change efforts were driven by university scholars whose pedagogy was informed by the theory that learning was a process in which students "discover not only knowledge of the subjects, but also the thought processes and methods of inquiry by which that knowledge is constructed."[3] Thus, these scholars called for the redefinition of teacher's and students' roles so that teachers became coaches while students were seen as active learners. While most innovations embodied this progressive theory of education, due to the absence of a clear and articulate theory of action of how to put these changes into practice, large scale innovations were rarely implemented successfully.

During the 1960s, educational research and practice functioned and operated as a technical process.[4] Educational research on school innovations exhibited The Guba and Clark model[5] known as the "Classification Schema of Processes Related to and Necessary for Change in Education." This consisted of four stages: Research → Development → Diffusion → Adoption (R, D, & D). In the research stage, knowledge was gathered for development. In the development stage, a solution to the identified problem was

1. Sarason, *Barometers of Change*, 47.
2. Elmore, *Restructuring in the Classroom*.
3. Ibid., 11.
4. Berman, *Three Perspectives on Innovation*.
5. House, *Technology Versus Craft*.

The Innovation and Diffusion Period

built. In the diffusion stage, the innovation was introduced to the practitioners. Finally, in the adoption stage, the innovation was to be incorporated in the school. The major proponent of the R, D, & D approach across disciplines claimed that the diffusion of an innovation or reform was a sequential process that followed an S-shaped curved.[6] In addition, Havelock (1971)[7] noted the assumptions of this R, D, & D change model as having a "rational sequence in the evolution and application of an innovation; planning usually on a massive scale; a division and coordination of labor; a more-or-less passive but rational consumer who will accept and adopt the innovation."[8] This R, D, & D rational approach functioned and was governed by the technological-experimental (TE) paradigm where "educational change was a problem amenable to technological solutions and schooling could be improved if tested and replicable products (technologies) were disseminated widely to schools."[9] Educational research and practice focused "on the innovation itself, its characteristics and component parts and on how to produce and introduce the innovation."[10] In short, educational reform was predominantly seen as a technical, rational, and linear process and imposed by external experts in the scholarly disciplines.

Two key and now classic studies during the early 1970s confirmed the assumptions that underpinned research and practice on school innovations and their consequences. Both of these studies were concerned with organizational innovations. One investigated the implementation of the catalytic model,[11] a curricular innovation aimed at altering the teacher-pupil relationship. The other studied the creation of the Kensington School,[12] an organizational

---

6. Rogers, *Diffusion of Innovations*.
7. Havelock, *The Change Agent's Guide to Innovation in Education*.
8. Ibid., 10.
9. Ibid., 257.
10. House, *Technology Versus Craft*, 28.
11. Gross, et al., *Implementing Organizational Innovations*.
12. Smith and Keith, *Anatomy of Education Innovation*.

innovation rooted in the new and progressive elementary education model.

In both of these cases, one of the factors that influenced the implementation process of organizational or curricular innovations was that teachers did not have clarity regarding the goals of the innovation and the means to enact those goals. In their study on the adoption of the catalytic role model (curricular innovation) at the Cambire school, researchers noted that "teachers never obtained a clear understanding of the innovation."[13] The catalytic model was intended to target "the problems of motivating lower-class children and of improving their academic achievement."[14] The catalytic model was designed to allow, encourage, ensure, and help children become intrinsic, self-motivated, responsible, competent learners in a changing society. Given these objectives and assumptions, under the catalytic model, the goal of the innovation was to redefine the teacher's role as one who "assisted children to learn according to their interests," "to emphasize the process, not the content, of learning," and to "function as a catalyst or guide."[15] Despite these intentions, teachers did not have a clear picture of what and how they were expected to implement the catalytic model. When asked about their understanding of the goal and the means of implementing the catalytic model in their respective classrooms, most teachers responded in terms of the new types of behavior to be adopted and behavior to be abandoned.

For example, teachers mentioned that the catalytic model demanded that they give children "freedom to choose activities, offer multiple activities, and individual attention," and "tolerate noise."[16] On the other hand, teachers mentioned that the catalytic model expected them to abandon the teaching of "formal lessons and group recitations" and "serve as authority figures."[17] Teachers faced enormous difficulties explaining and acting on the goal and means

---

13. Gross, et al., *Implementing Organizational Innovations*, 123.
14. Ibid., 10.
15. Ibid., 12–13.
16. Ibid., 124.
17. Ibid.

The Innovation and Diffusion Period

of the catalytic model. While they could talk and show what pupils should be doing, however, they could not talk about "specific behavioral requirements of the catalytic model with respect to their performance."[18] These findings supported the fact that planning for the implementation of the catalytic role model was inadequate, or worse, nonexistent.

In our second study,[19] researchers also noted that although users had a well-described statement of goals, they were not able to articulate its practical aspects. Within this organizational innovation, a school in a lower class suburban school district in a large metropolitan area in the Ohio River valley contracted an architectural firm to design a school that would represent and have embedded the "new elementary education of team teaching, individualized instruction, and multi-age groups."[20] The curriculum had an emphasis on "process development as opposed to content development. There was to be no one, central focus such as textbook-centeredness, pupil-centeredness, or teacher-centeredness; instead, numerous facets of the school were to shape the learning environment. Learning was viewed as an interactive process that varied from individual to individual."[21] The Kensington innovative school also included the redefinition of teacher-pupil roles. In order to socialize the faculty with its new role, the teachers would meet for four weeks—the summer workshop—before the start of the school. Organizationally, the Kensington School had three divisions: Basic Skills, Transition, and Independent Study (ISD). Each division had a distinctive function, multiple and varied means of achieving that function, a basic unit of organization, a specific organizational structure, and differentiated means for measuring pupil progress. On its institutional plan, the elementary school sought to "assist pupils to become fully functioning mature human beings," "meet the needs of individual differences," and "provide skills . . . which will enable pupils to identify worthwhile goals for

18. Ibid., 126.
19. Smith and Keith, *Anatomy of Education Innovation*.
20. Ibid., v.
21. Ibid., 33.

themselves, and to work independently."[22] Despite this statement of goals and structures, users were not able to articulate the operational plans of the Kensington innovation due to various conflicts. Users experienced a tension between the superintendent's call and view to build a school, the principal's institutional plan, and their own educational views.

Another source of conflict was the highly formalized educational doctrine. Due to its newness and to the perceived weaknesses of American education at the time, the district leadership saw the need to define and codify the educational doctrine at Kensington. The result of this action led to a doctrine that was abstract, wide in scope, complicated, unique, and too rigid. Staff conflict, difficulties in procedures, and incongruence with community were the outcomes. This all led to a façade or an image that the school used as "a cloak or screen covering the realities of organizational practices."[23] Goals were stated. However, the means to achieve those goals were not provided. As the authors concluded, "Common guidelines that guided did not exist; the language of school organization, teaching and goals for pupils remains metaphorical and literary but neither practical nor scientific."[24]

In addition to failure of clarity, a related factor that weakened the implementation process in the innovation and diffusion era was the restricted nature of the planning that preceded and the feedback that accompanied the implementation. Researchers,[25] for example, noted that teachers reported no specific differences in their conceptions of the catalytic role model between November, when the innovation was announced, and January when they were first asked to implement the model in their classrooms, a pattern that largely persisted into April.

Similarly, in the case of the Kensington innovation, teachers were expected to create and implement a curriculum rooted

22. Ibid., 32.
23. Ibid., 40.
24. Ibid., 53.
25. Gross, Giacquinta, and Bernstein, *Implementing Organizational Innovations*.

The Innovation and Diffusion Period

in individualized instruction, but were not introduced to it until four weeks before the official opening of the school. At this time, in a summer workshop teachers were trained by representatives of the National Training Laboratory. This was a "unique kind of learning experience in which a number of persons meet together and the activity of the group develops out of the growing relationships among the members of the group. The training was intended to make individuals more perceptive of group processes and their own personal relationships within the group."[26] However, these four weeks generated and crystallized several conflicts. One of these had to do with "substantive" versus "process" staff orientations. In the training process, primary attention was given to substantive concerns. The focus of planning became the institutional plan's mantra to help children become "fully functioning mature human beings."[27] During the four weeks of planning, curriculum subcommittees could not reconcile the dilemma highlighted by the administration's expectations to build a "totally individualized child-selected curriculum as opposed to a structured and sequenced set of experiences formulated by adults"[28] and on the other hand the administration's discouraging and intolerant attitudes toward critical or different points of view about the innovation among the staff. To illustrate, a staff member of the ISD division was immediately removed when it was discovered that his views were different from the team and blocked the functioning of the team as well. Instead of planning and providing an open space for the Kensington faculty to have authentic dialogue about the practical implications of pupil autonomy and individualized instruction in the classroom, the summer workshop highlighted the assumptions of the implementers and blocked the development and nurturing of a professional and collaborative educational climate.

In addition to problems of clarity and planning, both of these cases highlighted how the characteristics of the user could present

26. Smith and Keith, *Anatomy of Education Innovation*, 58.
27. Ibid., 66.
28. Ibid., 70.

a significant barrier to the implementation process during the innovation and diffusion period. Researchers at Cambire noted that teachers "did not possess the capabilities needed to perform in accord with the new role model."[29] Teachers reported facing several problems at different times during their efforts to implement the catalytic role model. Most teachers reported having serious difficulties, lacking the help they needed to carry out their new roles, while problems during the initial phase persisted.

Teachers also reported facing several other difficulties that arose during their efforts. Some of these included discipline issues, minimal learning, low interest and motivation of children, pupil misuse of materials and ineffective interaction with colleagues. It was thus concluded that teachers at Cambire were unable to develop and execute the competencies under the catalytic role model. At Kensington teachers experienced great difficulties enacting their roles in the innovative teacher-pupil relationships, especially in terms of defining and facilitating pupil responsibility in relation to the scheduling of classes in a new building. Another crucial factor that undermined implementation during the innovation and diffusion period was the poor quality as well as absence of appropriate materials. Teachers at Cambire did not have the required instructional materials, while the director made very clear that in order for teachers to act as catalysts, "they must make available to their pupils curriculum materials that are highly motivating and self-instructional in nature."[30] Teachers indicated that available materials were inadequate: "They hardly represent instructional materials that would permit a pupil to progress very far in a meaningful way on his own."[31] In short, at Cambire it was not only deficiency in the quantity but also the quality of materials that undermined implementation of the catalytic model.

On the other hand, researchers also noted that the alternative of grandeur in the sense of simultaneous whole school change

---

29. Gross, et al., *Implementing Organizational Innovations*, 129.
30. Ibid., 136.
31. Ibid., 137.

The Innovation and Diffusion Period

that was employed at Kensington[32] placed heavy demands of time and energy on teachers. The changing of multiple components and structures at the same time led to an increase of unintended consequences, heightened uncertainty, and excessive demand on both internal and environmental resources.

The final factor that affected the implementation process in both of these cases was leadership or management. At Cambire,[33] researchers documented "the failure of the administration to recognize or to resolve problems to which it exposed teachers when [it] requested them to implement the innovation."[34] The implementation strategy of the Cambire director required the explanation of the philosophy and objectives of the catalytic role model, the granting of freedom to teachers to implement the innovation, the delegating of responsibility, and the availability of additional funds. It was also reported that this strategy failed because difficulties arose when the innovation initiated by teachers was not taken into account and no mechanisms were made available to deal with unanticipated problems. Potential obstacles were not identified. Feedback mechanisms and opportunities to voice concerns and disagreements about the catalytic role model were largely suppressed. The director's assumptions regarding the operation and functioning of the catalytic role model at Cambire negated the identification of issues and facts that could have helped the director cope with the factors of implementation mentioned above.

On the other hand, researchers noted that at Kensington[35] the upside-down authority structure negated the work of democratic school administration. The traditional view of the district central office, the principal's inability to delegate responsibility, his role as a statesman, and his hyper-rationality in planning led to several consequences. Some of these included the costs translated into staff conflict and hostility, changing personnel, new organizational structures, confusion in handling pupils, and pupil dissatisfac-

32. Smith and Keith, *Anatomy of Education Innovation*.
33. Gross, et al., *Implementing Organizational Innovations*.
34. Ibid., 191.
35. Smith and Keith, *Anatomy of Education Innovation*.

tion. In short, the management strategy employed at Kensington triggered problems and issues that were counter to the egalitarian and democratic ethos that the educational innovation was intended to observe in the first place.

The innovation and diffusion period introduced major curricular and organizational innovations to schools. The general intended goal was to educate children so they were able to compete in a world that was in a global and competitive economy, technology, and scientific world. However, innovations were only initially/partially adopted. Innovations were not fully implemented because goals and the means to enact these, planning, roles, resources, and management were not articulated operationally or enacted culturally. The organizational realities of the schools did not reflect the actual description of the innovation. By the end of this era, it was becoming clear that the implementation of educational change was a neglected process.

Michael Fullan's Assessment on the Innovation and Diffusion Period

One of the scholars who pointed to the massive failure of educational innovations in early educational research and practice was Michael Fullan. In the early 1970s he noted that the R, D, & D approach to educational change had certain problematic assumptions regarding the role of the user.[36] This model assumed that innovations were developed and tested by experts, users were treated as passive receivers "either accepting or rejecting packaged innovations," and that innovations "could readily be accepted into a user system."[37] Change was viewed as a subject in which certainty was measured by quantitative and experimental methods. Fullan explained that the failure of the innovation and diffusion period stemmed from the educational research assertion that "to measure school innovativeness was to ask individuals how many specific

36. Fullan, *Overview of the Innovative Process*.
37. Ibid., 4.

The Innovation and Diffusion Period

innovations (from a predefined list) they had adopted over a given time period."[38] The focus was on the innovation, not the user. Fullan claimed that "there was little awareness that innovations require unlearning and relearning and create uncertainty and concerns about competencies to perform these new roles."[39]

Lack of attention to the complexities of using innovations in actual practice was the missing link. To respond to the challenge of the neglected user in the implementation process, the following elements of effective educational change processes at the user level model were suggested: user's objectives → adoption of sound innovations → user's acceptance → user's capabilities → effective outcome. The implications of this model called for close examination of the role of teachers in the change process.

It was concluded that "radical change can come only through the steady development of individual's capacities to play active roles."[40] Teachers had to play an active role in the change process. Their capacity and skill were crucial to the implementation of the change initiative. Unfortunately, teachers were expected to implement the adopted change in exactly the same manner that it was announced and prescribed. Worse, there were almost no mechanisms of communication or feedback between those choosing the initiative and those called to implement it in their corresponding classrooms.

A major review of curriculum reforms[41] affirmed the importance of closely looking at implementation to ensure that educational change has taken place. "We simply do not know what has changed unless we attempt to conceptualize and measure it directly; to understand some of the reasons why so many educational changes fail to become established; failure to do so may result in implementation being ignored, or else being confused with other aspects of the change process such as adoption (decision to

38. Ibid., 5.
39. Ibid., 15.
40. Ibid., 218.
41. Fullan and Pomfret, *Research on Curriculum and Instruction Implementation*.

use an innovation), or even the confusing of the determinants of implementation itself."[42]

A distinction was also made between implementation studies that had a fidelity perspective where the aim is to "determine the degree of implementation of an innovation in terms of the extent to which actual use of the innovation corresponds to intended or planned use"[43] and those that had a mutual adaptation which is "directed at analyzing the complexities of the change process vis-à-vis how innovations become developed/changed."[44] This major review basically argued that the implementation process takes place along the characteristics of the innovation strategies, characteristics of the adopting unit, and characteristics of macro sociopolitical units. Implementation is a process that should take into account local agents and/or users. They are the ultimate decision-makers. Thus, it is at the local level that implementation takes place. However, this study does not suggest "that local users determine all innovation decisions."[45] The implementation process should be the focus, and relationships must be re-defined. "We are saying, however, that if implementation is to occur on a wider scale, different aspects of the innovation process must be emphasized and a different basis for central/local relationships and process must be developed."[46] These claims sought to broaden the focus on innovation by highlighting to policy-makers and researchers the complexities of the implementation process. Implementation was looked at as a process in a social system affected by relationships and users.

Large-scale innovation during the innovation and diffusion period faced serious difficulties because of predominant technical assumptions. Implementation was expected to take place without attention to the user, and thus the unraveling and logical unfolding and unanticipated consequences and uncertainties. While Fullan's

42. Ibid., 337–38.
43. Ibid., 340.
44. Ibid.
45. Ibid., 393.
46. Ibid.

The Innovation and Diffusion Period

scholarly commentary never led a change period, it provided a perspective at the end of the period of why certain initiatives (within the period) succeeded and others did not. Change was assumed and treated to be a rational and linear process. The absence of a clear and articulate theory of action implied that adoption equaled implementation. The gap between the statements behind progressive practices and realities in the classroom documented by studies in the 1970s led a series of reform movements whose source was predominantly external and structural, as the next chapter shows.

2

School Effectiveness and School Improvement

In an effort to respond to the alarming failure of large scale innovations during the 1960s, educational researchers focused on finding what made schools effective as well as how they could improve. While the predominant issue during the 1960s was the innovativeness of educational reform driven by a response to Sputnik and a desire for national superiority, the overriding strategy since the 1970s had been twofold: to identify the characteristics of effective schools and their impact on pupil outcomes and to pinpoint the processes of change that schools needed in order to become better. The former refers to the school effectiveness knowledge base, while the latter refers to the school improvement practice base.

This chapter briefly reviews the research traditions of school effectiveness and school improvement. I will first outline their origins, aims, assumptions, and missions. I shall then explore their definitions and models and highlight Fullan's critical assessment of school effectiveness. Finally, the features of school effectiveness and school improvement are described in order to show the features that can bring them together. Two action research projects that illustrate attempts to link school effectiveness and school improvement are briefly described in order to then capture some of the unresolved issues that characterize these paradigms.

Origins, Aims, Assumptions, and Missions

The genesis of the school effectiveness movement in both the USA and Britain can be traced back to significant evaluation and reports of failed innovations during the late 1960s that claimed that home, family background, and socioeconomic status, not schools, determined student success.[1] It is critical here to acknowledge that the purpose of Coleman's report was to provide a basis for President Johnson's policy on school desegregation and for increasing support for schools serving high poverty communities. Coleman did not start out to document the failure of prior innovations in the early 1960s. He basically tried to identify inputs and outputs and found that schools inputs of any kind made little or no statistical difference in student outcomes.

In addition to these accounts, others similarly suggested that "education cannot compensate for society";[2] that hereditary reasons explained academic achievement;[3] and that social inequalities were at the root of underachievement.[4] While all of these claims illustrated the different ways that schools did not make a difference, the one thing that they held in common was that "they all vastly underestimated the influence of school on pupil progress."[5]

In the United States, the policy implications and practical consequences of the claims in the Coleman report were so disturbing that the education community started to raise significant questions regarding what schools actually could do to make a difference in the lives of disadvantaged students. Researchers then "began to look inside the school trying to assess how new

    1. Coleman, *Equality of Educational Opportunity*; Plowden, *Children and Their Primary Schools*.
    2. Bernstein, *Education Cannot Compensate for Society*.
    3. Jensen, *How Much Can We Boost IQ and Scholastic Achievement?*.
    4. Bowles and Gintis, *Schooling in Capitalist America*.
    5. Hopkins, *School Improvement in an Era of Change*, 43.

curricular, pedagogical and organizational ideas were organized, how teachers worked with students and with each other and what the role of leadership was."[6] These questions led to optimism about the impact of schools on children and to the birth of the school effectiveness movement. Inspired by the phrase "all children can learn," the school effectiveness movement[7] claimed that schools made a difference in the lives of disadvantaged children when they were characterized by five factors: strong administrative leadership, school climate conducive to learning, high expectation of children's achievement, clear instructional objectives for monitoring student performance, and emphasis on basic skills instruction.

School effectiveness was defined as the ability of the school to raise student outcomes beyond what their socioeconomic and family background variables would have predicted. Thus, a suburban school serving predominantly privileged and stable families would be expected to produce high student outcomes and would not therefore, according to the definition of effectiveness, be considered effective unless these students performed significantly above what would be expected. An urban school, however, with modest student test scores in basic skills might be considered effective because its students would be seen as achieving beyond what might have been expected given their socioeconomic backgrounds.

On the other hand, the school improvement paradigm is a direct response to the failure of top-down education reform in the 1960s. Top down education reform was predominantly guided and governed by the technological paradigm. Educational innovations were brought by people outside the schools, especially university professors, and based on the paradigm of expert knowledge in the academic disciplines at the highschool level and child development at the elementary level. These curricular and organizational innovations were primarily directed at student outcomes, focused on the school more than the teacher, and were grounded in a quantitative rather than in a qualitative paradigm.[8] The result of

6. Lieberman, *The Growth of Educational Change*, 16.
7. Edmonds, *Effective Schools for the Urban Poor*.
8. Reynolds, *Linking School Effectiveness Knowledge and School*

the documented failure of this top-down technological view of educational reform led to the birth of the school improvement paradigm. "The failure of 'top-down' approaches to educational change led to 'bottom-up' approaches that involved practitioner rather than external knowledge. The focus shifted from the educational organization as a unit for change to changes in educational processes."[9] In short, while the school effectiveness movement was a challenge to the prevailing educational discourse that schools did not make a difference, the birth of the school improvement paradigm was a reaction to an education reform approach that lacked teacher ownership and treated educational reform and change as an event, rather than as a process.

Thus, school effectiveness and school improvement not only represent different responses to the failure of large-scale educational innovations in the 1960s, but also contrasting aims:

> School effectiveness researchers have examined the quality and equity of schooling in order to find out why some schools are more effective than others in promoting positive outcomes . . . School improvement researchers have focused their studies on the processes that schools go through to become more successful and sustain this improvement.[10]

These aims imply that school improvement rests on a set of different assumptions from those of school effectiveness. School improvement practice operates under the following assumptions: the school as the center of change; a systematic approach to change; the internal conditions of schools as a key focus for change; accomplishing educational goals more effectively; a multi-level perspective; integrative implementation strategies; and the drive towardinstitutionalization.[11] In contrast to school improvement, school effectiveness has been historically grounded

---

Improvement Practice.

9. Fink and Stoll, *Educational Change: Easier Said Than Done*, 305.

10. Stoll, *Linking School Effectiveness Knowledge and School Improvement Practice*, 51.

11. Hopkins, *School Improvement in an Era of Change*.

on "a pragmatic response to policy initiatives; a commitment to quantitative methods; a concern with the formal organization of schools rather than with their more informal process; a focus upon outcomes which were accepted as being a 'good' that was not to be questioned and a focus upon description of schools as static, steady-state organizations generated by brief research study."[12]

Consequently, school effectiveness and school improvement have different missions.[13] School effectiveness is heavily research-based on outcomes and school improvement is innovation-based. For school effectiveness research "there are no time limits, while school improvement is an answer to a question requiring immediate action."[14] School effectiveness is also focused on developing theories and research results to gain quantifiable, objective knowledge about causes and effects, while school improvement is focused on change and problem solving strategies in order to gain subjective knowledge of how the individuals involved in reform manage to accomplish educational goals. Yet another difference concerns its methodology. School effectiveness researchers use rigorous statistical techniques for data analysis, while school improvement researchers have a "more developmental character; do not always begin with a well-phrased question and do not always end with a clear answer to that question."[15] Finally, school effectiveness researchers mainly focus on change in pupil outcomes and classroom level processes, while school improvement researchers expand their focus to include other factors and variables beyond the school level, such as school context. A discussion of the models advocated by each movement will provide an understanding of how these assumptions and missions have impacted educational reform and change.

12. Ibid., 57.
13. Creemers and Reezigt, *School Effectiveness and School Improvement*.
14. Ibid., 399.
15. Ibid., 400.

School Effectiveness and School Improvement

Models

In order to capture the theories and models that characterize school effectiveness and school improvement, it is imperative to start by defining them. In its basic and original form, the school effectiveness knowledge base is outcomes- and equity-oriented[16] while school improvement practice is process-oriented. That is, the former seems to be concerned with identifying those correlatives or predictors of students' academic achievement, the "what" of educational change, while the latter represents a "systematic sustained effort aimed at change in learning conditions and other related internal conditions in one or more schools, with the ultimate aim of accomplishing educational goals more effectively,"[17] or the "how" of educational change. In short, school effectiveness is about the ends, and school improvement is about the means of educational change. Although this may be a rather simplistic way to characterize these two movements, it nonetheless provides a framework to start examining their evolution as approaches to educational change.

As previously mentioned, the school effectiveness knowledge base began with the five factor model.[18] It was argued at the time that if schools adopted these principles, then educational goals would be accomplished. Despite successfully challenging the "school makes no difference" thesis and thus highlighting the importance of equity in schools, this model had several limitations. Edmond's five factor model was limited due to "its emphasis on basic skills, its assumption of causality based on correlational evidence, the independence and locus of factors and the tautology of relating an emphasis on basic skills to achievement in basic skills."[19] It is important to point out that it was under Edmonds' principalship that his school produced the results in student outcomes. It is thus critical to recognize that Edmonds did not set out

---

16. Levine and Lezzotte, *Unusually Effective Schools*.
17. Van Velzen, *Making School Improvement Work*, 48.
18. Edmonds, *Effective Schools for the Urban Poor*.
19. Stoll and Fink, *School Effectiveness and School Improvement*, 38.

with a five factor model. This model was developed by studying what Edmonds did as a principal. Measures of basic skills were the critical measure of effectiveness then. However, critics did not call for abandoning basic skills, but for going beyond them.

In its place, the five factor model was expanded and replaced by two significant studies: Fifteen Thousand Hours[20] and School Matters.[21] Fifteen Thousand Hours, a study of twelve secondary schools serving disadvantaged children in South London, aimed at answering if different schools had different effects on children's progress and, if this was the case, then to identify what makes some schools more successful than others. The findings in this study revealed that schools showed considerable differences in terms of delinquency rates, behavior patterns, attendance, and academic achievement. What was most striking about this study was that the schools "most likely associated with positive outcomes had created a particular ethos: a positive view of young people and of learning."[22] This implied that individual actions or means could have been combined to create a particular ethos or set of values and expectations that will characterize the school as a whole.

On the other hand, School Matters, a longitudinal study of primary schools, aimed at documenting the progress of a cohort of students from ages seven to eleven to establish the reasons as to why some schools are more effective than others and to find out differences in the progress of pupils, having taken into account variations in their intake characteristics. Similarly to Fifteen Thousand Hours, this study revealed that primary schools were also uneven in their effects. School Matters identified twelve key factors for effectiveness: purposeful leadership of the staff by the head teacher; the involvement of the deputy head; the involvement of teachers; consistency among teachers; structured sessions; intellectually challenging teaching; work-centered environment;

---

20. Rutter, et al., *Fifteen Thousand Hours*.
21. Mortimore, et al., *School Matters*.
22. Ibid., 88.

limited focus within lessons; maximum communication between teachers and pupils; record keeping; parent involvement; and positive climate.[23]

Fifteen Thousand Hours and School Matters significantly supported and deepened the thesis that "schools make a difference" and expanded the five factor model. They demonstrated that "most factors which emerged as being strongly associated with positive outcomes fell within the control of principals and teachers and few appeared to be determined from outside of the school."[24] In essence, what these studies accomplished was to replace the simplistic input-output framework embodied by the original correlates of achievement which were the parameters established by earlier research, with a much more rich and complex context-input-process-output model. Other attempts to expand this focus on context and process include an explanation of situational and contextual variables using contingency theory.[25]

In addition to these studies, other researchers have sought to broaden the contributors and variables and definitions of effectiveness. For example, some outlined what they deemed the most important organization-structure variables for effective schools.[26] These included school-site management, instructional leadership, staff stability, curriculum articulation and organization, school-wide staff development, parental involvement and support, school wide recognition of academic success, maximizing learning time, and district support. Furthermore, other scholars have also identified eleven factors for effective schools: shared leadership, shared vision and goals, a learning environment, a concentration on teaching and learning, high expectations, positive reinforcement, monitoring progress, pupil rights and responsibilities, and purposeful teaching.[27] In short, school effectiveness studies have

23. Rutter, et al., *Fifteen Thousand Hours*, 250–66.
24. Mortimore, et al., *School Matters*, 88.
25. Scheerens, *Effective Schooling*; Teddlie and Stringfield, *Schools Make a Difference*.
26. Purkey and Smith, *Effective Schools*.
27. Sammons, et al. *Key Characteristics of Effective Schools*.

grown from the simple five factor model into an extended and expanded list of variables and models.

In contrast to school effectiveness, school improvement researchers are very reluctant to provide models. Rather, school improvement practice offers perspectives, frameworks, guidelines ,and approaches.[28] School improvement researchers advocate for these instead of models because their aim is to demonstrate that educational change is a process, not an event.

Two key studies that illustrate this process-based definition of educational reform and change are Innovations Up Close and Improving the Urban High School. Innovations Up Close was a multi-case study of 12 chosen sites within a large sample of 146 sites or schools from suburban, rural, and urban settings. It aimed to "develop explanations, a reasonable web of causal influences that help us understand, not just that a school improvement effort worked or failed in the special circumstances at the [chosen sites], but why it did."[29] Using ethnographic methods, researchers reported that the adoption of an innovation was heavily influenced by multiple motives that were strongly related to career plans, the centrality of classroom life, and the initial attitude toward the program. The key finding of this study was that school improvement requires confronting several dilemmas: fidelity versus adaptation; centralized versus dispersed influence; coordination versus flexibility; ambitiousness versus practicality; change versus stability; and career development versus local capacity.[30]

On the other hand, Improving the Urban High School, an in-depth multi-case study of five highschools located in major American metropolitan cities, was guided by the argument "that creating more effective schools requires a significant change in

---

28. Ainscow, et al., *School Improvement in an Era of Change*; Caldwell and Spinks, *The Self-Managing School*; Fullan, *The New Meaning of Educational Change*; Hopkins, *School Improvement in an Era of Change*; House, *Three Perspectives on Innovation*; Joyce, *The Doors to School Improvement*.

29. Huberman and Miles, *Innovations Up Close*.

30. Ibid., 278–80.

patterns of leadership and management at the school level."[31] Researchers argued that school improvement required that the old model (organizing for stability), a bureaucratic one due to its "clear division of labor among people in different roles and to its clear hierarchy,"[32] needed to be replaced by a more adaptive model, one that is predicated upon the "need for constant learning and evolution to improve the basic functioning of the school."[33]

The key finding of this study was that there are certain action motifs that successful and effective change leaders and agents must follow. Change leaders must articulate a vision. "Effective school leaders are able to talk about what they want for the school"[34] and "help people develop images of 'how to get there' which are process themes."[35] They also get shared vision ownership—"sharing responsibility and accountability."[36] And, ". . .staff should be rewarded for suggesting and trying new things, not only for succeeding,"[37] as well as use evolutionary planning—"not a hand-to-mouth approach, but coherent, intelligent adaptation based on direct experience with what is working toward the vision and what isn't."[38] On the other hand, change agents must negotiate the school's relationship and its environment. As environmental managers, effective school agents require that change agents be" proactive by grabbing, getting, and taking advantage of potential resources rather than waiting for them to be provided; think constantly of assistance, training, and support as a master resource that will help other staff; think very broadly about resources and extend the traditional teacher-buffering activities of principals to include a more active negotiating stance in relation to the district

31. Louis and Miles, *Improving the Urban High School*, 19.
32. Ibid., 22.
33. Ibid., 26.
34. Ibid., 30.
35. Ibid., 31.
36. Ibid.
37. Ibid., 31.
38. Ibid., 32.

office."[39] In addition, change agents have coping skills. In order to obtain and achieve these skills, change agents are called to "coordinate and orchestrate the evolution of the program within the school" and be "deep copers"[40] by having "enormous persistence and tenacity"[41] and to have a "high tolerance for complexity and ambiguity."[42] In sum, school improvement requires the adoption and articulation of a shared vision and image, evolutionary planning, effective relationships, resources, and coping skills.

The findings of these two school improvement studies demonstrate that there is no recipe or single solution that can help schools get better. Rather, school improvement researchers provide evidence that the development of effective schools and effective teaching is a process full of contradictions and dilemmas.

Coming Together: The Legacies of School Effectiveness and School Improvement

Despite having different intellectual orientations and missions, researchers have pointed out that school effectiveness and school improvement need each other's approaches, perspectives, and findings.[43] In fact, school effectiveness and school improvement not only complement each other, but also their corresponding shortcomings can be counterbalanced by their separate strengths:

> School effectiveness researchers can provide knowledge for school improvers about factors within schools and classrooms that can be changed to produce high-quality schooling, whereas school improvement strategies

39. Ibid., 33.
40. Ibid., 34.
41. Ibid., 35.
42. Ibid., 35.
43. Clark, et al., *Effective Schools and School Improvement*; Creemers and Reezigt, *School Effectiveness and School Improvement*; Gray, et al., *Merging Traditions*; Lezotte, *Base School Improvement on What We Know About Effective Schools*; Reynolds, et al., *Linking School Effectiveness Knowledge and School Improvement Practice*.

provide the ultimate test for many of the theories posited by school effectiveness researchers.[44]

Building and sustaining links between school effectiveness and school improvement demands an examination of their respective legacies. This chapter examines the possibilities of merging these two movements by listing their contributions and the ways they complement each other.

The school effectiveness knowledge base has made a number of significant contributions to the study of change in schools. Researchers in school effectiveness focused on outcomes and equity. Historically, the quality of education in the United States has been dependent on wealth and socioeconomic status. As a result, educational achievement has been directly associated with resources (input). School effectiveness researchers have challenged this prevailing view by highlighting what schools can do to make a difference in student outcomes. School effectiveness has also demonstrated that despite divergent socioeconomic backgrounds, all students can learn and achieve, but not necessarily with equal results.[45] Researchers of school effectiveness have redefined school success "not in absolute success but as the value added, beyond wealth and family background influences, to what students brought to the educational process" and claimed that "effectiveness depended on an equitable distribution of learning outcomes across the entire population of the school."[46]

In contrast, school improvement researchers rarely focus on outcomes, and at times this focus on process often appears as a goal in itself and neglects an impact on student learning by "underemphasizing the end of the chain."[47] In the age of accountability and multiple innovations, school improvement researchers can use the characteristics of effective schools to test their strategies for accomplishing educational goals. School improvement researchers

44. Stoll, *Linking School Effectiveness and School Improvement*, 55.
45. Edmonds, *Effective Schools for the Urban Poor*; Nuttall, et al., *Differential School Effectiveness*; Teddlie and Stringfield, *Schools Make a Difference*.
46. Murphy, *The Educational Reform Movement of the 1980's*, 95.
47. Hopkins, et al., *School Improvement in an Era of Change*, 39.

can be informed by the historical emphasis on equity of the school effectiveness movement. School improvement researchers should also be "aware of the background of the student population in a school before they assess the value added by the school's change effort over and above what the students might be expected to learn given their background, prior knowledge, and attitudes."[48]

In addition to a focus on outcomes and equity, researchers in school effectiveness have embraced the use of data for decision-making and provided knowledge of what is effective elsewhere. Due to its outcomes-based research and practice orientation, school effectiveness "offers a database to help schools in their own planning."[49] School effectiveness helps schools determine where they are by identifying their needs. The use of data can help school improvement researchers to determine what strategies and approaches are meeting the needs of different student population groups. In addition, the school effectiveness knowledge base provides schools with a list of characteristics of effective schools that has been evolving over the years and in which there is significant overlap. Consistent findings of school effectiveness studies conducted over time can also guide school improvement researchers in the reaffirmation and reformulation of frameworks, processes, strategies, and approaches to educational change.

Researchers in the school effectiveness movement have also emphasized that the school is the focus of change. Educational change should have a school-based orientation. As was mentioned earlier, top-down education reform was unsuccessful because it treated educational change as a large, technical matter. It did not take into account the people that study and work in schools as well as the unique contextual characteristics. School effectiveness researchers stress that "individual schools need to take responsibility for their own change efforts."[50] The school as a focus of change can inform school improvement researchers of the need to appreciate

---

48. Stoll, *Changing Our Schools*, 55.
49. Ibid., 56.
50. Ibid.

and determine those strategies and processes of change that may work in one context (secondary), but not in another (elementary).

Researchers in the school improvement paradigm have also made a number of significant contributions to the study of educational change. School improvement researchers claim that educational change is a process and that it is permeated by an orientation toward action and ongoing development. School improvement researchers have focused on providing assistance regarding the change process. Specifically, researchers within this tradition have pointed to the phases of change: initiation, implementation, and institutionalization. Building on these findings, school improvement researchers have argued that due to the dynamic nature of schools as institutions, approaches to educational change should not aim at imposing specific solutions. Schools are constantly changing, therefore "only by studying this process of change and its impact can we really understand schools."[51] School effectiveness researchers should take into account that educational change is a process, not an event and that teacher ownership is critical. Thus, researchers in school improvement can help broaden effective school characteristics by adopting a process orientation that encompasses teacher outcomes as well as a progress orientation that includes the evaluation of children across multiple outcomes.

Another contribution of the school improvement movement to the study of educational change includes an emphasis on school-selected priorities for development. School improvement researchers point out that one of the major reasons why early educational change efforts failed often was due to a lack of ownership at the user level. Therefore, school improvement practice highlights the need of engagement on the part of teachers directly responsible for implementing educational innovations at schools. Various school improvement approaches such as school development planning and the doors to school improvement represent deliberate and practical actions and projects that highlight the critical importance of involvement and ownership of the process of change. Given its emphasis on school-selected priorities for

51. Ibid., 57.

development, school improvement researchers' expertise can be useful in the application and translation of school effectiveness characteristics.

In addition to selected-school priorities, researchers in the school improvement tradition have tried to get inside the black box of educational change by examining the impact and role of the school culture. Recently, school improvement researchers have focused on the potential of the school culture to develop and nurture or inhibit a climate of trust and collaboration that is conducive to continuous learning. A focus on culture informs and guides school effectiveness researchers in their quest for relevance and usefulness.

School improvement researchers can help school effectiveness researchers broaden their definitions by adopting a multilevel perspective on characteristics. On one side, school improvement researchers view the school as the centre of change. This implies that education reform should be context-sensitive. One size does not fit all. On the other side, a school "cannot be separated from the context around it."[52] Schools need to be part of a wider context under which they operate.[53] Schools need to make connections to other schools and districts as well as universities, community organizations, and businesses.

The legacies of school effectiveness and school improvement feature a series of components that can be used to make closer links between the two. School improvers can be provided with the factors that build capacity to improve instruction that, in turn, enhance student learning. School effectiveness researchers can be provided with the strategies to field test effective characteristics. One area of inquiry where these two paradigms have come together is action research.

---

52. Ibid., 58.
53. Sirotnik, *Ecological Images of Change*.

Combining School Effectiveness and School Improvement

Two action research projects that illustrate the linking of the school effectiveness and school improvement paradigms are the Halton Effective School Project and Improving the Quality of Educational for All (IQEA). The Halton Effective School Project was an "attempt to bring the results of school effectiveness research carried out within Britain (Mortimore, et al., 1988) into the schooling practices of Canada."[54] However, due to the difficulties found in the implementation of the project, a school improvement approach was adopted to generate and inform change strategies.

> Essentially, top down mandates to schools to address the characteristics of effectiveness failed because they did not engender ownership and commitment, nor did they pay attention to the process and impact of change on those who worked through it.[55]

Building on the school improvement literature, Halton was based on the assumption that the school is the center of change. This meant that the school was not viewed as an isolated entity, but as connected to the wider community. Halton was also guided by a strategic plan in which the district played a significant role. This strategic plan included a school growth planning process consisting of four stages, namely, assessment, planning, implementation, and evaluation. a focus on instruction, where the district established student outcomes and the staff development. The purpose of this strategic plan was to build a system that "provided a framework within which growth planning could occur and offered support for success."[56] This was the significant role of the district in Halton.

Halton's model of school effectiveness was measured by the use of questionnaires. Through these parents, students and teachers were able to offer an assessment of where the school was in

---

54. Stoll and Fink, *Linking School Effectiveness and School Improvement*, 55.

55. Ibid., 58.

56. Ibid., 59.

reference to clear indicators. In addition, schools were also encouraged to examine curricula and instructional strategies and education initiatives emanating from the Ontario Ministry of Education.

Halton's key finding was that school growth planning led to greater staff involvement, a collaborative culture and the collective building of a vision among teachers and principals. Researchers found that the "growth planning process showed that the creation of an effective school depends on much more than the knowledge of what has been successful and effective elsewhere."[57] In short, process strategies are shaped by the unique context of the school.

The IQEA project, involving a number of schools belonging to the English Local Education Authorities, aimed at equipping schools with the resources to provide quality education for all. Similarly to Halton, IQEA seeks to combine the school improvement and school effectiveness paradigms. IQEA is "pupil orientated, involves measurement of program success or failure at outcome level but is also concerned with the within-school study of school processes from a qualitative orientation."[58] IQEA was based on the assumptions of enhanced outcomes, the role of the school culture, school background and organization as key factors, a clear and practical focus for development, a simultaneous focus in the conditions as well as the curriculum, and a strategy that links priorities to the conditions.

The key finding of IQEA is that improvement strategies work best "when a clear and practical focus for development is linked to simultaneous work on the internal conditions of the school."[59] In the IQEA project, schools use the impetus of external reform to enhance student outcomes. Schools identified priorities, created internal conditions, and selected strategies. These strategies included staff development, inquiry and reflection, leadership, coordination, and collaborative planning. What is significant about

57. Reynolds, et al., *Linking School Effectiveness Knowledge and School Improvement Practice*, 48.
58. Ibid.
59. Ibid.

School Effectiveness and School Improvement

the IQEA project is that it employs a holistic strategy (curriculum, conditions, strategies etc.) to accelerate the achievement of students and the improvement of schools' conditions.

The two projects briefly described above demonstrate that it is possible to link the school effectiveness knowledge base and school improvement practice. These two paradigms do not have to be mutually exclusive. They can complement each other. A close examination of the legacies of these paradigms and possibilities for a fruitful union are provided. The Halton and IQEA projects represent two examples of this possible merger. School effectiveness can provide the knowledge of those factors that can be manipulated by change strategies. School improvement can provide the change strategies that can be used to test the factors identified by school effectiveness. However, questions regarding the relevance and implementation of characteristics of effective schools as well as the measurement of improvement projects remain critical issues to be dealt with before close links can be made between school effectiveness and school improvement.

The main task here is to combine school processes with student outcomes. Some issues that remain unsolved in this task are whether the characteristics of effective schools remain relevant today as well as whether they can be implemented. The school effectiveness knowledge base runs the risk of becoming irrelevant due to the fact that "key studies carried in the 1970s and 1980s are largely based on what makes schools effective in the here and now, not what is necessary in a fast changing world."[60] School effectiveness studies can also become irrelevant due to the narrow and decontextualized measures of student outcomes employed and relied upon which can perpetuate "instruments of social inequity and educational reductionism."[61]

In terms of whether the characteristics of effective schools can be implemented, the pressing issue is that schools deal with multiple innovations and represent "unique cultures, contexts,

---

60. Fink and Stoll, *Educational Change: Easier Said Than Done*, 303.
61. Ibid., 303.

macro and micro-politics."[62] The message here is that there is a strong need for "multidisciplinary, multi-leveled descriptions of schools and their communities as complex, interrelated non-linear systems that can help inform educational change efforts."[63]

One last issue to be addressed in the merging of school processes and student outcomes is how to measure the impact of school improvement projects. There are two issues here. One is how to measure the progress of a school toward a chosen focus. Another is how to measure the change process itself. The former is about the attainment of student outcomes. The latter concerns the evaluation and monitoring of specific school improvement strategies. The challenge was how to ensure that student progress and outcomes were reached without sacrificing school and teacher quality. This tension highlights the potential contributions that a merging between the school effectiveness and school improvement paradigms brings to the study of educational change.

The failure of large-scale innovations in the 1960s was followed by the birth of the school effectiveness and the school improvement movements. School effectiveness began by challenging the thesis that schools do not make a difference. School improvement represented a direct response to the top-down education reform approach of the 1960s. The former aimed at identifying the characteristics of effective schools and its impact on pupil outcomes while the latter aimed at illuminating the processes schools undergo in order to become better.

Fullan's Assessment of School Effectiveness and School Improvement

Thus, school effectiveness and school improvement have historically operated under different assumptions and been guided by distinct missions. In fact, school effectiveness advocated for models that identified correlatives for effective characteristics,

---

62. Ibid., 304.
63. Ibid., 304.

while school improvement researchers called for guidelines and frameworks.

The impact of school effectiveness is narrow and limited due to the neglecting of process factors and variables. School effectiveness "has mostly focused on narrow educational goals, and the research itself tells us almost nothing about how an effective school got that way and if it stayed effective."[64] Moreover, organization-structure variables are limited.[65] Process variables should be treated as means to achieve organizational factors. That is, organization-structure variables should be accompanied by process factors in order to fuel the dynamics of interaction and development. These included: leadership feel for the improvement process, the presence of an explicit implemented value system, intense interaction and communication, and collaborative planning and implementation. The idea is that school improvement is the result of the combination of organization-structure and process factors. Educational change is not only about effectiveness and outcome factors, but also about improvement and process factors.

The field of educational change has advanced as a result of the development of the school effectiveness knowledge as well as the school improvement practice bases. Clearly, the unresolved issue in efforts to merge these two stemmed from the tension of outcomes and processes. The 1980s dealt with this tension by calling for a reexamination of the schools in terms of their structural and cultural issues. Thus, educational change now turned to restructuring and reculturing.

---

64. Fullan, *The New Meaning of Educational Change*, 22.
65. Purkey and Smith, *Effective Schools*.

3

Restructuring and Reculturing

Since the early 1980s, efforts to improve public schools have generated various approaches to bringing about educational change. Two of these were school restructuring and reculturing. This chapter examines the legacy of these two vehicles of school improvement. It first outlines the antecedents of school restructuring. Then it explores the origins, meanings, and strategies of school restructuring as well as key studies. Following school restructuring, this chapter explicates school reculturing by investigating the origins and types of culture, describing the advocates, meanings ,and models of school culture as well as several of its key theoretical and empirical analyses and studies. Finally, Fullan's assessment of school restructuring and reculturing is explored in order to capture his contribution within this period.

Antecedents of School Restructuring

The antecedents of the current movement to restructure schools can be traced back to controversial national commission reports and privately funded studies during the early 1980s.[1] The most

---

1. Jacobson and Conway, *Educational Leadership in an Age of Reform*; Murphy, *The Educational Reform Movement of the 1980's*.

Restructuring and Reculturing

influential of these was the report of the National Commission on Excellence in Education (NCEE): A Nation at Risk.[2] This initiated what is known as the first wave of reforms (1982–1985) and the beginning of the excellence movement which operated under the assumption that problems in education "were traceable to low standards for workers and low quality of production tools."[3] Therefore, A Nation at Risk pointed to the failure of the American education system and the risk that this posed to the nation's democratic and economic well-being. The NCEE supported these claims by citing international comparisons of student achievement, highschool and adult illiteracy rates, and SAT scores. In order to correct these deficiencies, A Nation at Risk made five major recommendations: content, standards, and expectations; the expansion of time; new approaches on teaching and learning the basics; the reconceptualization of leadership; and strengthening fiscal support. It was recommended that highschool students take a significant number of courses in the five new basics: English, math, science, social studies, and computing. It was also recommended that K-12 and higher education institutions "adopt more rigorous and measurable standards, and higher expectations, for academic performance and student conduct,"[4] and that "significantly more time be devoted to learning the New Basics,"[5] as well as that major steps be taken for the improvement of "the preparation of teachers or to make teaching a more rewarding and respected profession."[6]

Despite awakening millions of Americans to a "crisis" in elementary and secondary education, A Nation at Risk did not produce fundamental changes. "Recommendations were often vague, only weakly linked to empirical knowledge about teaching and learning and noncommittal to implementation."[7] For example, recommendations on curricular content urged attainable goals,

2. *A Nation at Risk: The Impetus for Educational Reform.*
3. Ibid., 22.
4. *A Nation at Risk: The Impetus for Educational Reform.*
5. Ibid.
6. Ibid.
7. Jacobson and Conway, *Educational Leadership in an Age of Reform*, 9.

namely, the increase in course requirements in English, math, social studies, science, and computer science. However, little was proposed about "teaching students and teachers the skills they must know to work effectively with academic content."[8] Similarly, recommendations for higher standards for student performance reasserted the value of traditional grades and standardized tests of achievement while ignoring "the issue of grade inflation or the difficulty of developing uniform, usable criteria for determining appropriate standards for grading."[9] In short, A Nation at Risk was written under the assumption that the existing system was basically sound, and that schools could be improved by fine tuning and by simply doing more of what they already did. The chief goal of these Wave 1 reforms was to restore excellence and quality by fixing the system in a mechanical and standardized manner.[10] The underlying common philosophy of Wave 1 reforms was "that the conditions of schooling contributing to poor student outcomes are attributable to the poor quality of the workers and the inadequacy of their tools and that they are subject to revision through mandated, top-down initiatives—especially those from the state."[11] The policy mechanisms used to improve schools were simplification, prescription, and performance measurement.

Origins, Meanings, and Strategies of School Restructuring

The genesis of school restructuring was a result of the consensus among the education and policy community that Wave 1 reform measures were insufficient.[12] Educational reformers concurred that there was a need for "a fundamental revision in the way schools

---

8. Ibid., 9.
9. Ibid.
10. Murphy, *The Educational Reform Movement of the 1980's*.
11. Ibid., 2.
12. Chubb, *Why the Current Wave of School Reform Will Fail*; Elmore, *Reformed and Culture of Authority in Schools*.

were organized and governed."[13] For example, the Carnegie Forum of Education and the Economy in their report A Nation Prepared stated: "We do not believe the educational system needs repairing; we believe it must be rebuilt to match the drastic change needed in our economy if we are to prepare our children for productive lives in the 21st century."[14]

Known also as Wave 2 reforms, school restructuring was guided by the assumption that "problems are traceable to systems failure."[15] School restructuring, therefore, implied a shift from the bureaucratic model of control and compliance perceived to be rooted in centralized top-down mandates to a radical change of governance and work structures through bottom-up initiatives.

While there is no single meaning of restructuring, the central idea implies some sort of fundamental change in the way that schools are organized and in the way they operate. Restructuring strategies include school-based management, choice, teacher empowerment, and teaching for understanding. For the Carnegie Forum on Education and the Economy, restructuring entailed changes in teacher professionalism, autonomy, and career rewards and changes in the structure toward placing decision-making authority near those at the schools. The National Governors Association also proposed the redesigning of curriculum and instruction to promote teaching for understanding; decentralizing of decision making to the local school; differentiating the roles of teachers; and providing a variety of accountability strategies.

Across the different dimensions of restructuring, all proposed strategies encompass one or more of three specific models: the technical model that seeks changes in the way teaching and learning occur or in the core technology of schooling; the professional model that seeks changes in the occupational situation of educators, inclusive conditions of entry, and licensure of teachers and administrators along with changes in school structure, conditions of work, and decision-making processes within schools; and

13. Murphy, *The Educational Reform Movement of the 1980's*, 25.
14. Ibid., xx.
15. Ibid., 2.

the client model that seeks changes in the distribution of power between schools and their clients or in the governance structures within which schools operate. Based on these strategies and models, the educational and policy community designed and enacted various restructuring initiatives or reforms at the local, district, and national levels.[16]

Key School Restructuring Studies

A case study of restructuring experiments in three urban elementary schools was conducted to investigate the idea that education and policy makers "can change how teachers teach and how students learn by changing the ways schools are organized."[17] Researchers provided case analyses of the literary, scientific, and mathematical practices of four individual teachers at each school.

The researchers found that all three schools restructured successfully. They changed the way students were grouped; provided time for teachers to meet and share knowledge by working in teams; accessed new ideas through professional development opportunities; enacted a common vision of student learning; and acquired greater responsibility on matters that had been decided in the past by the district or the state. Schools also exhibited major differences. All schools were different in the length of the change process, the district environment, teaching practice, and knowledge. The key finding of this study was that changing teaching by changing the structure of the organization is a relationship that is "weak, problematic and indirect"[18] because "structural change often detracts from the more fundamental problems of changing teaching practice."[19] No "single set of structural changes that schools can make will lead predictably to a particular kind of

16. Berends and King, *A Description in Restructuring in Nationally Nominated Schools;* Datnow, et al., *Extending Educational Reform;* Fullan, *The Return of Large-Scale Reform;* Newmann and Associates, *Authentic Achievement.*
17. Elmore, *Restructuring in the Classroom,* 1.
18. Elmore, *Restructuring in the Classroom,* 237.
19. Ibid.

teaching practice."[20] Likewise, it is "just as plausible for changes in practice to lead to changes in structure as vice versa."[21] Changing teaching practice is "fundamentally a problem of enhancing individual knowledge and skills."[22] In sum, this study affirmed the complexity of teaching and the importance of recognizing that since good teaching practice involves addressing the nature of learning explicitly, the structural conditions that can foster it are important but not sufficient for educational change.

A second study aimed at documenting the impact of restructuring initiatives in schools and youth-serving community agencies on the life chances of disadvantaged youth.[23] This study claimed that "unless restructuring is directed at the school's core cultural beliefs and values affecting the quality of students' experiences and teachers' work lives, the modification of mere organizational structures will have little payoff in terms of better outcomes for students."[24] The study reported on the impact of various interventions in several long-term structural reforms, which included site-based management and teacher empowerment, extensive staff development training activities, and ways of collaborating and coordinating with other organizations and agencies.[25]

This study concluded that long-term structural reforms were not sufficient to stimulate the restructuring of schools. Interventions did not bring about fundamental change, change the core of classroom activities, engender greater faculty investment in their schools, or fully develop the linkage needed between stakeholders and schools to improve social relations. In sum, this study indicated that structural changes in schools and youth-serving community agencies were not successful because they represented supplemental programs that left the basic experiences of students and teachers unchanged.

20. Ibid., 238.
21. Ibid., 239.
22. Ibid., 240.
23. Wehlage, et al., *Restructuring Urban Schools*.
24. Ibid., 54.
25. Ibid., 58.

A third study reported on how restructuring efforts impact the quality of instruction and achievement for all students. This synthesis of four studies was conducted by the University of Wisconsin-Madison sponsored Center on Organization and Restructuring of Schools from 1990 through 1995. It focused on a variety of restructuring strategies: site based management and shared decision making; students and teachers organized in teams; multiyear instruction on advisory groups of students; heterogeneous groupings of students in core subjects; and enrollment based on student and parental choice.[26] The scholars found that organizational changes in schools did not necessarily address the quality of student learning. "New administrative arrangements and teaching techniques contribute to improved learning only if they are carried out within a framework that focuses on learning of high intellectual quality."[27] This occurred when students were allowed and encouraged to construct knowledge "through disciplined inquiry to produce discourse, products and performances that have value beyond certifying success in school."[28] Three kinds of supports were crucial for this kind of student learning: authentic pedagogy, school organizational capacity, and external support by agencies and parents.

These key studies demonstrate that structural reform does not necessarily lead to change in teaching, institutional and student learning practices. Core beliefs and values about the inner world of teaching and learning remain largely untouched. At the same time, student as well as adult learning is inhibited by the organizational context of teaching in terms of its traditional and outmoded structures. Partly in response to these and other limits, the school improvement movement evolved from an emphasis on procedures and formal processes such as school development planning to focus more on the study of school culture[29] in terms

26. Newmann and Wehlage, *Authentic Achievement*.
27. Ibid., 51.
28. Ibid.
29. Fullan, *Changing Forces*; Hargreaves, *Changing Teachers*; Hargreaves, *Cultures of Teaching: A Focus for Change*; Hargreaves, *Cultures of Teaching and*

of the role of beliefs, relationships, commitments, and motivations in change efforts.

Origins and Levels of the Concept of Culture

The concept of culture originates from anthropology, psychology, sociology, and corporate world theorists and researchers. An organization's culture refers to "the deeper levels of basic assumptions and beliefs that are shared by members of an organization, that operate unconsciously, and that define in a basic 'taken-for-granted' fashion an organization's view of itself and its environment."[30] Culture is the "invisible, 'taken-for-granted' flow of beliefs and assumptions that gives meaning to what people say and do"; "shapes how they interpret hundreds of daily transactions and is reflected and transmitted through symbolic language and expressive action consisting of the stable underlying social meanings that shape beliefs and behavior over time."[31] Culture is also viewed as both a product and process.[32] As a product, culture refers to the accumulated wisdom of the past. As a process, it undergoes constant renewal and recreation as newcomers learn the old ways and eventually become teachers themselves. Organizational culture is simply explained as "the way we do things around here." In sum, culture is the sum total of assumptions, values, norms, beliefs, and expectations that have emerged and evolved over time in a specific organization or context.

There are three levels of culture: artifacts, values, and basic assumptions.[33] These measures depend exclusively on the degree of visibility to the researcher. Artifacts refer to the physical and social environment. Artifacts include the school's physical space, its dress and language, climate, stories, rituals, myths, and cer-

---

Educational Change.
30. Schein, *Organizational Culture and Leadership*, 6.
31. Deal and Peterson, *Shaping School Culture*, 3.
32. Bolman and Deal, *Reframing Organizations.*
33. Schein, *Organizational Culture and Leadership.*

emonies. At a more complex level are espoused values and beliefs. According to Schein, as these problems develop, they are solved. For example, when a faculty faces a problem, the group decides on a course of action or solution. Basically, a choice is made based on some sort of assumption as to what will eventually work or not. When this course of action or solution becomes, through repeated choices, an effective way to solve a particular problem, then this converts into a shared value or belief that is often taken for granted. These solutions then become the accepted norms and rules of behavior that will dictate and predict the actions that make and end up in artifacts. The problem with these shared values and beliefs is that they often tend to be forgotten with the passage of time and thus people continue to profess ideals they do not practice; hence they are called "espoused" values. At an ever deeper level than both artifacts and values are basic assumptions. These are the most unconscious, implicit, invisible, and invincible elements of culture. Assumptions are harder to pinpoint than the artifacts that are highly observable when one walks into schools. They are hardly confronted and thus almost impossible to change. Facing the assumptions that govern actions demands the reexaminations of beliefs that make up the conservative and stable configuration of people's cognitive structure. In short, culture can be best described by understanding and exploring three levels: artifacts, values, and basic assumptions.

Advocates, Meanings, Models of School Culture and Teacher Cultures

Partly in response to the limits inherent in restructuring as a sole strategy of educational change, researchers and writers in the school improvement tradition have shifted their focus toward the study of school culture.[34] The complexity of school culture is underscored by the multitude of ways it has been defined. For

---

34. Fullan, *Change Forces: Probing the Depths of Educational Reform*; Hargreaves, *Cultures of Teaching*; Hargreaves, *Changing Teachers, Changing Times*; Hargreaves, *Cultures of Teaching and Educational Change*.

example, school culture is defined as "a structure, process, and a climate of values and norms that channel staff and students in the direction of successful teaching and learning."[35] School culture is a "complex pattern of norms, attitudes, beliefs, behaviors, values, ceremonies, traditions and myths that are deeply ingrained in the very core of the organization."[36] It has also been described as the guiding beliefs and expectations that are clearly evident in the way that the school operates, particularly in the manner people relate to each other.[37] School culture is being described as "being embedded in people's attitudes, values, and skills, which in turn stem from their personal backgrounds, from their life experiences, and the communities they belong to."[38] In sum, while there is no single universal meaning of school culture, the central approach is to examine and uncover those less tangible, implicit, and unspoken aspects that guide the beliefs and relationships of students, teachers, and principals within schools.

But what then is the role of school culture in school improvement? The existence and critical role of school culture has been widely documented. Early on, sociologists affirmed and stressed the organizational culture of schools: "Schools have a culture that is definitely their own. There are, in the school, complex rituals of personal relationships, a set of folk ways, mores, and irrational sanctions, a moral code based upon them. There are games, which are sublimated wars, teams, and an elaborate set of ceremonies concerning them. There are traditions and traditionalists waging their old-world battle against innovations."[39] More recently, the necessity of attending to the cultural dimensions of schooling has been highlighted when it was documented that "student learning gains have been associated with a handful of school characteristics without convincing rationales and empirical support for how

---

35. Purkey and Smith, *Effective Schools*, 64.
36. Barth, *The Culture Builder*, 7.
37. Hargreaves and Fullan, *What's Worth Fighting for In Your School?*
38. Senge, *The Fifth Discipline*, 325–26.
39. Waller, *The Sociology of Teaching*, 96.

it affects the internal dynamics of schools."[40] In short, research reveals the existence of a school culture and of its critical role in student achievement, teacher learning, and school improvement.[41]

Researchers also point out different models of school culture sthat can help educators identify the degree to which their particular schools are developing and improving. For example, researchers have claimed that school culture is expressed in four ways: moving, cruising, strolling, and sinking schools. The argument here is grounded on two dimensions, namely, effective, ineffective ,and improving-declining.[42] Moving schools are not only characterized as effective in "value added" terms but consist of a staff that is able to respond to the changing context and to further development. Cruising schools are described as effective organizations by multiple stakeholders and through various standardized data. However, these schools reflect and reinforce the 1965 nostalgia and model of education and therefore are unable to allocate time to prepare pupils for a rapidly changing world. Strolling schools are neither effective nor ineffective. These are governed by contradictory aims and goals that frustrate efforts at both effectiveness and improvement. Struggling schools are considered ineffective but improving in the sense that they may have the will but not the skill to change. Networks and consultants can facilitate skills development in struggling schools. Finally, sinking schools are both ineffective and unable to improve. These schools are not only undermined by previous historical and cultural traditions, such as isolation, self-reliance, blame, functions that inhibit improvement, but also by lower SES characteristics and by a discourse that places school failure on families and children.

Another model through which school culture can be examined embodies one of two domains: instrumental and expressive.[43]

40. Rosenholtz, *Teacher's Workplace*, 2.
41. McLaughlin and Talbert, *Contexts That Matter for Teaching and Learning*; Sarason, *The Culture of the School and The Problem of Change*; Sarason, *The Predictable Failure of Educational Reform*.
42. Stoll and Fink, *Changing Our Schools*.
43. Hargreaves, *Changing Teachers, Changing Times*.

Restructuring and Reculturing

The instrumental domain is based on social control while the expressive domain reflects social cohesion. Grounded in a high-low continuum, school cultures are classified into five types: (1) traditional (low social cohesion, high social control, which are custodial, formal, unapproachable; (2) welfarist (low social control, high social cohesion), which are relaxed, caring, cozy; (3) hothouse (high social control, high social cohesion), which are claustrophobic, pressured controlled; (4) anomic (low social cohesion, low social control), which are insecure, alienated, at risk; and (5) effective (optimal social cohesion, optimal social control), which have fairly high expectations, support for achieving standards. The point of these models is not to locate a particular solution within a specific model but to initiate a discussion to identify aspects that are distinctive of school culture, especially aspects which affect student learning. The models may suggest appropriate strategies teachers and principals can use to shape school culture in the name of student learning and professional development.

In addition to these two types of school culture, the educational change literature has gone further to investigate the significance of teacher cultures. A distinction is made distinguishing between the content and the form of teacher cultures.[44] The content of teacher cultures "consists of the substantive attitudes, values, beliefs, habits, assumptions and ways of doing things that are shared within a particular teacher group, or among the wider teacher community," while the form of teacher cultures "consists of the characteristic patterns of relationship and forms of association between members of those cultures."[45] The form of teacher cultures may be individualization, balkanization, collaboration, and contrived collegiality. In the culture of individualism, teachers work independently and in isolation from each other; teachers display orientation of presentism, conservativism, and individualism.[46] In the culture of balkanization, teachers are separated and united by the loyalties and identities that they attach to particular

---

44. Hargreaves, *Cultures of Teaching*.
45. Ibid., 219.
46. Lortie, *School Teacher: A Sociological Study*.

groups of their colleagues. In a culture of collaboration, teachers work together and share ideas. "Collaborative cultures require broad agreement on educational values, but they also tolerate disagreement, and to some extent actively encourage it within those limits."[47] Finally, cultures of contrived collegiality are characterized by mandated, imposed, and regulated initiatives. Some of these may include mentor coaching, peer coaching, joint planning, and scheduled meetings. The significance of teacher cultures is that these dictate where teachers learn to teach and influence the kind of teacher they will become.

Models of school culture and teacher culture highlight the need for educational research and practice in the name of student learning. Rather than offering solutions, these can ignite a discussion as to what factors and challenges educators and policy makers face when striving to increase student achievement. Those challenges may point to a concerted effort at reculturing the school. The next section examines some of these issues.

Reculturing: Theoretical and Empirical Studies on School Culture

Based on various empirical and theoretical studies and analyses, researchers and writers have argued for the reculturing as well as restructuring of schools.[48] One of the most critical issues in the reculturing literature is the superficiality of change when the effort is based on a vocabulary of crisis or reform employed by federal and state policy makers. The contradiction of long-term stability amid constant change is inherent in schooling improvement.[49] He claims that change does not necessarily imply or mean progress. There are two kinds of planned change in school reform. One is first-order changes that will include, for example, the recruitment of teachers

---

47. Ibid., 226.

48. Elmore, *The Limits of Change*; Fullan, *Change Forces: Probing the Depths of Educational Reform*; Hargreaves, *Cultures of Teaching*; Hargreaves, *Cultures of Teaching and Educational Change*.

49. Cuban and Tyack, *Tinkering Toward Utopia*.

and the raising of salaries. The other is second-order changes that includes open classrooms and teacher-run schools. The distinction between these two changes explains the "durability that we find in the governance, pedagogy and structure of schooling."[50] In short, this analysis points out that attempts to reculture schools need to be reframed in questions of depth and extent of intended school reform that place in the foreground the goals of proposed changes as well as the history of previous efforts.

Another significant question within the reculturing literature is whether beliefs and relationships that shape reform are based on a bureaucratic view or professional approach. Scholars have convincingly argued that part of the solution to the problems that plague public education stem from the diminishing professionalization of teaching. The increasing centralization and bureaucratization of education is dehumanizing and constraining. It focuses on what is specific, measurable, and predictable, and therefore reduces school's responsiveness to distinctive student needs. The professionalism of teaching implies a more client-oriented and knowledge-based view for structuring schools and teaching practice. Attaining the conditions and benefits of professionalism requires changes in the preparation for and structuring of practices, new models of decision-making, and the allocation of resources. Professionalization of teachers develops responsibility and authority and accountability for student learning that are grounded on a redefined and broadened view of teaching as a profession characterized by continuous learning and reflection.

Similarly, scholars have documented the extent to which the bureaucratic conditions of the workplace impact the quality of teaching.[51] This inductive and exploratory study consisted of interviews of exemplary teachers nominated by their own principals from public, independent, and church-related schools. It aimed at gaining insight regarding how teachers experienced their schools as workplaces, the particular features that supported or compromised their best teaching and the changes they perceived

50. Ibid., 74.
51. Johnson, *Teachers at Work*.

were needed to help them become better. One significant finding of this study revealed that the professional status of teachers was circumvented. "Their special interests and expertise were neutralized; they were expected to comply rather than invent. They doubted their students' needs were well met."[52] Unsuitable and large bureaucratic structures included such elements as standardized testing, prescribed curricula, block schedules, and graduation requirements. In sum, this study concluded that the reculturing of schools requires that policy makers and administrators spend fewer resources on the formalization and standardization of education and more on permitting and promoting flexibility and adaptation.

A third challenge surfaced by researchers in the reculturing literature is how to cultivate and promote collaboration. In a study that describes the possibilities and limits of collegiality among teachers, scholars highlight how collaboration during which teachers mutually examine teaching and learning is rare. "Collaborative efforts run counter to historical precedent, tending to be unstable, short-lived and secondary to other priorities."[53] It also underscores that collegiality has both benefits and risks associated with it. It can be a means for coherence and uniformity as well as an instrument that can crush individual inventiveness and independent initiative. Institutional supports at all levels of the school and system are thus a necessary condition. Similarly, distinguishing between the form and the content of collegiality helps illuminate the value and significance of collegiality to alter beliefs and commitments in teaching as part of school reculturing efforts. This study affirms that forms of collegiality move from independent to interdependent points on a continuum as the demands and changes for collective autonomy and teacher-to-teacher initiative increase. Storytelling and scanning, aid and assistance, sharing and joint work constitute such forms. The issue is to recognize that they militate against the inherited traditions of non-interference and equal status. Thus, the motivation and reward to move from one form to another is found

52. Ibid., 144–45.
53. Little, *The Persistence of* Privacy, 187.

in the work of teaching and "not in the absence of interdependent work-related interests."[54]

The content or substance of collegiality is a result of the mutual influences among teachers. In this way, collegiality is an effect of unspoken teachers' values and beliefs about children which can either "advance the prospects for students' success or intensify norms unfavorable to children."[55] The intellectual dispositions and capabilities of teachers can represent "the creative development of well-informed choices or the mutual reinforcement of poorly informed habit."[56] Likewise, the commonalities held among teachers "may lead them to pursue new courses of action and support one another in the attempt—or gain together to preserve and reinforce the status quo."[57] That is, an emphasis on collegiality can promote either the potential benefit of allowing teachers to revisit and reexamine questions of teaching and learning or the reassertion and reinforcement of beliefs, norms, and relationships that confirm traditional norms of schooling. In short, this analysis indicates that an emphasis on collegiality to reculture schools does not automatically promote changes in teaching and learning always.

Similarly, other scholars expand the value and significance of collaborative structures for the reculturing of the teaching profession.[58] This study aimed at documenting the relationship between time, work, and culture in teaching. It was conducted in twelve elementary schools in two school boards in Ontario, Canada, where elementary teachers shared a minimum of one hundred twenty minutes or more of preparation time per week. The focus of this qualitative and exploratory study was "to investigate the meanings that teachers and principals attached to preparation time and other non-control time and the interpretations they put on its use."[59] The key question of this study was whether preparation time

54. Ibid., 523.
55. Ibid., 524.
56. Ibid., 152.
57. Ibid., 527.
58. Hargreaves, *Changing Teachers, Changing Times*.
59. Ibid., 121.

would lead to collaboration and collegiality among teachers or whether the use of such a time would be absorbed into the existing culture of individualism. Here it is revealed that the safe simulation of contrived collegiality dominated preparation time study. The properties and consequences of this pattern of teacher collaboration clearly emerged during mandated preparation time use, consultation with special education resource teachers, and peer coaching. "In contrived collegiality, collaboration among teachers was compulsory, not voluntary; bounded and fixed in time and space; implementation- rather development-oriented; and meant to be predictable rather than unpredictable in its outcomes."[60] The major consequences of contrived collegiality were inflexibility and inefficiency. The former referred to the difficulty of programs to fit to the purposes and practicalities of particular schools and classroom settings, thereby eroding teachers' professionalism and discretionary judgment. The latter referred to the reluctance and unwillingness of school and educational systems to delegate to their teachers substantial responsibility for the development and implementation of curricula. The unwillingness at the district, state, and national levels to un-write curriculum guidelines to allow teachers greater flexibility in their own work contributed to their inefficiency. This work highlights the fact that restructuring and reculturing are both crucial. It also illustrates that restructuring initiatives overshadow the reculturing of teaching which is often undermined and inhibited by politics and the bureaucratization of teaching.

The complexity of reculturing schools also stems from the political and normative dimensions of reforms. The study of the implementation of the Carnegie Council on Adolescent Development Turning Points' reforms of middle-grades schooling is a case in point.[61] This study sought to problematize the change and policy environment of the reform milieu and provide educators with "legitimate avenues for questioning the values and politics

---

60. Ibid., 208.
61. Oakes, *Becoming Good American Schools*.

Restructuring and Reculturing

that drive much contemporary school reform."[62] In doing this, this study described and analyzed the experiences of sixteen schools in five states that were trying to be more effective and embrace virtue through the creation of educative, socially just, caring, and participatory places for students grounded in the American traditions and legacies of Jefferson, Lincoln, Adams, and King respectively. Despite great efforts, it was concluded that "reform is a very fragile human process, not a technical one."[63] The schools in this study struggled with conventional policy implementation attitudes and norms steeped in instrumental and technocratic means and ends that treated teachers as passive and isolated consumers of knowledge and skills. As a result, new structures were adopted and enacted without giving attention to deeper beliefs and meanings. For example, many teachers serve on teams without inquiring about their nature, rationale, and meaning. One teacher explained how "everybody kind of jumps on the bandwagon and does them without really thinking about the process of change and how do we make that happen. Some people think that because they've changed the structure, they're there."[64] In short, Oakes, et al. concluded that reculturing schools is complex due to the fact that reform strategies and structures are often hierarchical, impersonal, normative, and seldom redefined and reexamined by teachers in terms of their potential and implications to change underlying beliefs and norms about teaching and learning.

One last critical issue within the reculturing literature is whether successful reforms can be spread from one school or district to others. "We can produce many examples of how educational practice could look different, but we can produce few, if any, examples of large numbers of teachers engaging in these practices in large-scale institutions designed to deliver education to most children."[65] This is known as the sustainability of

---

62. Ibid., xiv.
63. Ibid., xxiii.
64. Ibid., 242.
65. Elmore, *Getting to Scale*, 11.

educational change (or whether what matters spreads and lasts).[66] Several key studies document the difficulty of sustainability. For example, a study of the scaling up of comprehensive reform design models documents that the failure to sustain reform is a result of the actions of reformers in distant locations that are insensitive to the culture of the schools or the perplexities of the daily life of educators.[67] Similarly, a comparison of reform strategies in New York and San Diego highlights that the spreading of educational change depends on an appreciation of the political dimensions of reform that the learning demands from the reform, the size and pace for reforms and the degree of alignment between various cultural, organizational, and political elements and the programs that are advocated.[68] In sum, reculturing schools is exceedingly difficult due to the fact that transferability and sustainability (the breadth of reform in this case) is both a function and effect of contextual variations.

To recap, researchers in the field of educational change have shifted their focus toward the study of school culture. Known as reculturing, this is an attempt to study the beliefs, norms, and relationships that shape and guide the actions of people and institutions in order to understand cultures' influence on efforts to improve schools. Theoretical as well as empirical evidence highlights the complexity of reculturing schools. School reformers often fail to reculture schools because of the superficiality of change embodied in the rhetorical discourse used by top policy makers, the increasing bureaucratization of teaching, the risks associated with collegiality, the technical and hierarchical nature of reforms, and the lack of breadth of educational changes. But what then does Fullan say about the restructuring and reculturing of schools? The next section delves into his contribution during this period.

---

66. Hargreaves and Goodson, *Educational Change Over Time*.
67. Datnow, et al., *Extending Educational Reform*.
68. Stein, et al., *Reform Ideas That Travel Far Afield*; Oakes, *Becoming Good American Schools*.

Restructuring and Reculturing

Fullan's Assessment on Restructuring and Reculturing

In terms of school restructuring, structural strategies and reforms "do not struggle directly with existing cultures within which new values and practices may be required."[69] What is thus needed is the opportunity and skill for teachers to question and change their beliefs and habits. This signals the need for change capacity.[70] In other words, the problem of change is how to make the educational system a learning organization. Moral purpose and change agentry is at the heart of a learning organization.[71] The moral purpose involves educators' commitment "to make a difference in the lives of students regardless of background and to help them produce citizens who can live and work productively in increasingly dynamic complex societies."[72] The latter is to be "self-conscious about the nature of change and the change process."[73] Moral purpose is not only about personal caring and interpersonal sharing, but also about broader social, moral, and public responsibilities and purposes. Change agentry requires personal vision-building, inquiry, mastery, and collaboration. Experiencing and thinking about the change process demands the recognition of the normal nature of complexity, dynamism, and unpredictability. A new paradigm of dynamic change is thus based and predicated "on one's ability to work with polar opposites."[74] Finally, the ultimate purpose was to change schools from bureaucratic organizations into thriving communities of learners. This underscored the need for schools to live interactively with the environment, the importance of teacher education, and the role of inner and outer learning in helping teachers produce a learning society.

69. Fullan, *The New Meaning of Educational Change*, 25.
70. Fullan, *The Meaning of Educational Change*.
71. Fullan, *Change Forces: Probing the Depths of Educational Reform*.
72. Ibid., 4.
73. Ibid., 12.
74. Ibid., 40.

On the other hand, Fullan argues that reculturing schools demands attention to the elements that characterize the culture of teachers and schools, the need to go deeper and wider, and the need for leadership of the change process. One of the challenges of reculturing is the particular way teachers engage with each other as they work toward school improvement.[75] The way to promote teacher collegiality is to advocate for the totality of the teacher. This refers to the purpose, person, and context of the teacher. In addition to the totality of the teacher, there is a critical need to examine the totality of the schools. The guiding question is "what kinds of work communities or school cultures are most supportive of teacher growth and school improvement?"[76]

Moreover, reculturing depends on building connections between purpose, passion, emotion, hope, and structural initiatives.[77] This means going deeper. They also argue that there is a need to reframe relationships with the outside. In their own words, reculturing is facilitated when connections are created and cultivated with parents and communities, governments, technology, businesses, and teacher education institutions.

Reculturing schools requires new forms of leadership. At the school level, there is the non-rational and paradoxical world of the principal.[78] The world of the principal is a complex one full of conservative tendencies that "inhibit sustained attention to change."[79] He also urges principals to be cognizant of the fact that the system is unreasonable and thus full of uncertainties and dilemmas. Thus, the role of the leader is to capitalize on and "foster a climate where people are able to work with polar opposites; push for valued change while allowing self learning to unfold; see problems as sources of creative solution; have good ideas but not

---

75. Hargreaves and Fullan, *What's Worth Fighting for Out There?*.
76. Ibid., 37.
77. Hargreaves and Fullan, *What's Worth Fighting for Out There?*.
78. Fullan, *What's Worth Fighting for In The Principalship?*.
79. Ibid., 3.

be blinded by them; and strive for internal cohesion as they are externally oriented."[80]

At the policy level, the concept of reculturing implies mobilizing educators to reconsider and reexamine the beliefs and norms governing the delivery of instruction is not enough. "Development of individuals is not sufficient."[81] Relationships are crucial for school improvement but only if they establish greater program coherence and bring in resources. Thus, relationships are not ends in themselves. They can be positive or negative. In short, the role of leaders in reculturing is to cause greater capacity and coherence.

To summarize, it is essential to recognize the existence, value, and necessity of restructuring. However, this recognition does not necessarily lead to school improvement when there is no space for teachers and principals to question their beliefs as well as the values and norms that shape and guide their relationships. Reculturing requires attention to the culture of the schools as it affects its teaching and leadership force.

So far, I have attempted to examine the legacy of restructuring and reculturing as vehicles for school improvement. I have discussed the origins, models, advocates, and some of the strategies as they are shown in theoretical and empirical analyses and studies. While restructuring has been advocated by state and federal policy makers, reculturing is foregrounded by several theorists and researchers in fields such as the organizational psychology and corporate world.

As we have seen, restructuring reveals a lack of depth in school reform. It hardly gets to core issues in teaching and learning. On the other hand, reculturing underscores the lack of breadth of school reform. Reculturing is often undermined by bureaucracy and historical/contextual facts, many of which block the spread of reform. That is, while restructuring indicates the rationality and technical character of educational change, reculturing demonstrates the difficulties and complexities of changing beliefs and norms that are inherent in the historical, social, and political

80. Ibid., 16.
81. Fullan, *Leading in a Culture of Change*.

contexts of schooling. Fullan's scholarly commentary never led this change period but was somehow part of it and provided a perspective in the middle of the school restructuring and reculturing period that called attention to the superficiality of restructuring efforts. Teaching and learning values and practices remained largely intact. He advocated for the reculturing of schools. In addition to restructuring, Fullan argued for ignited moral purpose, a focus on total teachers and schools, and new conceptions of leadership.

4

Large Scale Reforms

Partly in response to the lack of depth and breadth of educational change in school restructuring and reculturing respectively, policy makers and researchers have adopted the systemic perspective.[1] Beginning in the 1990s, governments across the world began instituting large scale reforms.[2] Reformers turned their attention to improving the overall system. Rather than focusing on a single subject, grade, department, and school, entire school districts as well as states and countries became the unit of change. Large scale education reforms intended to go deeper and broader than previous isolated and specific (noted earlier under restructuring and reculturing) initiatives. That is, key issues in large scale reform constitute the conditions and action that are necessary to ensure that reforms are embedded and sustained beyond the initial conception, adoption, and implementation stages.[3] The extent to which progress or regress is reached or compromised under the current

 1. Smith and O'Day, *Systemic School Reform*.
 2. Fullan, *Change Forces: The Sequel*; Fullan, *The Return of Large-Scale Reform*; Fullan and Earl, *Implementation of National Literacy and Numeracy Strategies*; Leithwood, et al., *Large Scale Reform?*; Leithwood, et al., *A Framework for Research in Large Scale Reform*; Levin, *Inevitable Tensions*; Levin, *Sustainable, Large-Scale Education Renewal*.
 3. McLaughlin and Mitra, *Theory-Based Change and Change-Based Theory*.

climate and orthodoxy of standards-based education reform and high levels of consequential accountability remains to be seen.[4]

To examine the factors that promote and inhibit large scale education reform, this section highlights Fullan's contributions at the end. This chapter consists of four parts. Large scale reform is defined. Examples of large scale education reforms at the district and national levels are briefly described. Professional learning communities as a key strategy to the embedding (deepening) and sustaining (broadening) of large scale reform over time are described and analyzed. Finally, Fullan's writings on large scale education reform are highlighted in order to ascertain his contribution within this period.

Definition and Models of Large Scale Education Reforms

Although there is no universal definition of what large scale education reforms mean, it has been suggested that these initiatives focus on an "entire system where a minimum of 50 or so schools and some 20,000 or more students are involved."[5] Models of large scale education reform include the whole-school reform designs, school district, state/provincial reform, and national reform initiatives. Basically, large-scale reform is a system-wide strategy that attempts to bring change by articulating a clear theory of action.

Whole-school reform designs are also known as comprehensive school reform (CSR) models.[6] Success for All (SFA) is one example of a CSR model. SFA was created and established by Robert Slavin in 1987 and a team of researchers at John Hopkins University. Thus, SFA is a research-based design that organizes resources to focus on prevention and early intervention to ensure that

---

4. Earl, et al., *Large-Scale Education Reform*; Hargreaves, et al., *Learning to Change*. Hargreaves and Goodson, *Educational Change Over Time*; Hasser and Steiner, *Strategies for Scale*.

5. Fullan, *Building a New Structure for Leadership*, 8.

6. American Institutes for Research, *An Educators' Guide to School-Wide Reform*; Berends, et al., *Facing the Challenges of Whole-School Reform*.

students succeed in reading throughout the elementary grades. SFA consists of three programs: an Early Learning program for pre-kindergarten and kindergarten students; Reading Roots, a beginning reading program; and Reading Wings, its upper-elementary counterpart.[7] Major components of SFA are ninety minutes of daily reading instruction; eight week assessments; one-on-one reading tutors; cooperative learning; family support team; local facilitators for mentoring and counseling; staff supports for implementation; and training and technical assistance by SFA staff. SFA is guided by a theory of action derived from organizational and staff changes, family and community support, supplies and materials, a focus on curriculum and instruction, and the assessment of student progress and performance. In addition, SFA encourages districts and school staff to examine program materials and visit exemplary schools as well as require a vote of 80 percent of the faculty, a full-time facilitator, a certified teacher tutor and a family support team to engage in SFA.[8]

School District Reforms

Another example of large-scale reform is school district reform.[9] New York City District 2 is one of thirty-two community school districts. It has twenty-two elementary schools, seven junior highschools, and seventeen option schools, which represent alternative schools organized around common themes. District 2 serves a diverse student population. When in 1987 Alvarado became superintendent, the district ranked tenth in reading and fourth in mathematics out of a total of thirty-two community districts in NYC. In 1996, District 2 came in second place in both reading and mathematics. This success was attributed to Alvarado's strategy which was a set of organizing principles and staff development models. This set of organizing principles was accompanied by a

---

7. Slavin, et al., *Success for All*.
8. Slavin and Madden, *Disseminating Success for All*.
9. Elmore and Burney, *Investing in Teacher Learning*.

system-wide strategy that employed an embedded professional development theory of action model that included a professional development laboratory, instructional consulting services, inter-visitations and peer networks, off-site training, oversight, and principal site-visits. District 2 considered professional development as something administrators did rather than a specific and isolated task that was assigned to particular experts or departments. In sum, "professional development is a management strategy rather than a specialized administrative function."[10]

In addition to New York, the San Diego City Schools (SDCS) is another example of attempted school district reform.[11] SDCS is the eighth largest school system in the United States. During 2001–2002, it had 137,536 students. SDCS is a K-12 district with more than one hundred fifty schools. It serves a diverse student population of which most are Hispanic and twice the percentage of English language learners when compared to New York (28.4 percent in SDCS while 13.9 in District 2). During the early 1990s, SDCS was characterized as a decentralized, autonomous, reactive, and competitive system.[12] This resulted in the inequitable distribution of resources, information, and capacity across district clusters managed by multiple area superintendents. In the mid-1990s, the Greater San Diego Chamber of Commerce's Business Roundtable focused on education reform through changing the district leadership. As a result, in 1998, the Board appointed US attorney Bersin as superintendent and Alvarado as chancellor of instruction. Similar to New York District 2, SDCS reform was guided by a theory of action grounded in major organizational changes focusing on instruction. SDCS was reorganized into seven clusters. Each cluster consisted of twenty-five schools and was managed by area superintendents called Instructional Leaders (ILs). These ILs received specific and specialized training from the University of Pittsburgh's Learning Research and Development Center. ILs

10. Ibid., 272.
11. Stein, et al., *Reform Ideas That Travel Far Afield*.
12. Earl, et al., *Large-Scale Education Reform*.

Large Scale Reforms

were trained to coach and evaluate principals and monitor student performance.

In the spring of 2000, SDCS adopted The Blueprint for Student Success. This plan constituted a content-driven, centralized, comprehensive, and fast-paced reform. The focus was on literacy and mathematics. Central leadership initiated major changes in operations, instruction, and professional development. Reform changes were mandated and expected in all schools.

ILs conducted monthly conferences with their cluster school principals, and in turn principals conducted monthly meetings with their teachers. A partnership with the University of San Diego provided professional development to the district and school leaders. Weekly visits to schools, videotaping of principal conferences, walkthroughs, coaching, and problem-solving sessions were other mechanisms used at all levels of the systems.

Chicago Public Schools (CPS) is one more example of district reform.[13] This is the third largest school system in the United States. It has more than five hundred schools serving communities with very diverse populations. During the 1980s, a series of commission reports documented the decline of CPS in terms of its dropout rates and student achievement in multiple standardized tests. As a result, CPS adopted the Chicago Reform Act of 1989. This act was grounded in the idea of democratic government. This meant a "shift from centralized democratic control, exercised through a bureaucracy to expand local democratic control exercised through school councils."[14] The theory of action guiding CPs was one rooted in the principles of citizen participation, community control, and local flexibility. A complete reorganization of CPS shifted power and responsibility to local school councils (LSCs) from the Central Board of Education.

CPS reform was based on six principles. LSCs were established. Each LSCs consisted of eleven members. These included sixelected parents, two elected community members, two teachers, the principal, and one elected student member for highschools.

13. Bryk, et al., *Charting Chicago School Reform*.
14. Ibid., 17.

LSCs were responsible for evaluating, hiring, and firing principals and developing and approving the school improvement plan and budget. They also provided advice regarding school curriculum, instruction, and budget through the Professional Personnel Advisory Committee. The principalship was reshaped in terms of its authority over school staff and various incentives and sanctions. Principals were also able to recruit and hire new teachers; remove incompetent teachers; had more control over physical plant and ancillary personnel and more freedom regarding the use of discretionary money. Teachers had a greater role and influence in school decision making. Fiscal resources were redirected to the school level in order to generate equity across the system. Central Office expenses had a cap; budgets were implemented at the school level; funds were allocated in equitable ways to individual schools and high percentages of low socioeconomic students who received larger discretionary revenues. Central office authority was decentralized and curtailed. The authority of the Central Board of Education to appoint principals was eliminated. Their control over curriculum was restricted, and line control over regular school operations was eliminated. Finally, there was a centralized focus toward improving student learning. This included the creation and establishment of system-wide goals for student learning and school improvement; the development and updating of three-year school improvement plans; annual reports of progress; and a set of sanctions and external interventions intended to move forward nonimproving schools.

National Reform Initiatives

A key example of large scale at the national level is England's National Literacy and Numeracy Strategy (NLNS).[15] NLNS is both a response to as well as a result of changes in government and policy.[16] From 1979 to 1996 a conservative government came into

15. Barber and Seba, *Accountability vs. Autonomy*; Fullan, *The Return of Large-Scale Reform*; Fullan and Earl, *United Kingdom National Literacy and Numeracy Strategies*; Fullan, et al., *Implementation of the National Literacy and Numeracy Strategies*.

16. Earl, et al., *Large-Scale Reform*; Levin, *Reforming Education*.

power and began to enact legislation that resulted in substantial changes in educational policy. These included greater parental choice, local management of schools at the expense of powers of local authorities, a national curriculum, national assessment, a national system of school inspections (The Office of Standards in Education), the repeal of Labour legislation, signifying in part the ending of collective bargaining for teachers, and the creation of a teacher training agency which was directly appointed by the Education Secretary.

In 1997, the Labour government defeated conservatives in the general election. The NLNS thus began as an effort to establish literacy and numeracy as first order priorities. Using 1996 as the baseline (57 percent of eleven-year-olds achieved proficiency level in literacy, and 54 percent in numeracy, respectively), policy makers announced 80 percent for literacy and 75 percent for numeracy as targets. In order to move schools forward from their evidently underperforming status, the English government based its reform in a High Challenge: High Support model.[17] Capacity-building strategies were added and combined with the accountability mechanisms established by the previous conservative government.

Whether at the school, district, or national level, educational scholars claim that large-scale education reform is possible and it makes a difference in student learning, in teacher professionalism, and in generating public support. The lesson is the following:

> Large-scale, sustained improvement in student outcomes requires a sustained effort to change school and classroom practices, not just structures such as governance and accountability. The heart of improvement lies in changing teaching and learning practices in thousands of classrooms, and this requires focused and sustained effort by all parts of the education system and its partners.[18]

---

17. Fullan and Earl, *United Kingdom National Literacy and Numeracy Strategies*.

18. Levin, *Reforming Education*, 323.

One way to view the challenging nature of large-scale reform is to describe and question the pressing factors that facilitate both the embedding (deepening) and sustaining (broadening) of reform over time. One key factor and strategy advocated to deepen and embed large scale reform is the adoption and implementation of professional learning communities (PLCs).

Background Prior to Professional Learning Communities

During the 1980s, attention shifted toward a focus on both the corporate and public education worlds on how work settings influenced the quality of work and workers themselves. Scholars described and analyzed how business and private industry managers can pinpoint those cultural factors that promoted and inhibited change.[19] Scholars have underscored the role of the learning organization[20] particularly by emphasizing "the importance of nurturing and celebrating the work of each individual staff person and of supporting the collective engagement of staff in such activities as shared vision development, problem identification, learning, and problem resolution."[21]

Linking Large Scale Reforms to PLCs

One way to accomplish large-scale reforms and thus bring about improvement in learning at the school and district levels is to build professional learning communities. It is well documented that professional development contributes to school capacity that is the provision of knowledge and skills.[22] However, this approach may

---

19. Deal and Kennedy, *Corporate Cultures*.

20. Senge, *The Fifth Discipline*; Block, *Stewardship*; Whyte, *The Heart Aroused*.

21. Hord, *Professional Learning Communities*, 12.

22. Newman, et al., *Professional Development That Addressed School Capacity*.

be too individualistic and thus lack organizational development. It is exceedingly complex because it is like sending a changed agent into an unchanged institutional culture. Thus, school capacity is about both individual and organizational development. Schoolwide PLCs purports to seek ways to acknowledge and support how the environment and relationships can lead to better student outcomes.[23] A consistent focus on collaboration, teaching and learning, and assessment data can help accomplish large scale reforms.[24]

The concept of "Professional Learning Communities" (PLCs) consist of three foundational words.[25] "Professional" is someone that has received advanced training in his position and is thus responsible for remaining up to date in the changing knowledge base of that particular field. "Learning" points out the lifelong commitment of that individual to purposeful, ongoing study, along with habits of questioning, curiosity, and inquiry. Finally, "community" refers to "a group linked by common interests."[26]

Although there is no universal definition of PLCs, various researchers and theorists have attempted to define what it means or implies. One model[27] proposed three related communities: (1) the professional community of educators; (2) learning communities of teachers and students (and among students) both within and outside the classroom; and (3) the stakeholder community. A learning community is defined as "schools where the leaders have intentionally shaped the culture and acted to ensure that all mem-

23. Darling and Hammond, *The Quiet Revolution*; DuFour, et al., *Recurring Themes of Professional Leaning Communities*; DuFour and Eaker, *Professional Learning Communties at Work*; Hord, *Professional Learning Communities*; Louis and Kruse, *Professionalism and Community*; McLaughlin and Talbert, *Contexts That Matter for Teaching and Learning*; Scribner, et al., *Creating Professional Communities in School Through Organized Learning*; Wenger, *Communities of Practice*.

24. Huffman and Hipp, *Reculturing Schools As Professional Learning Communities*; Newmann and Wehlage, *Successful School Restructuring*; Newmann ,et al., *Professional Development That Addressed School Capacity*.

25. DuFour and Eaker, *Professional Learning Communities at Work*.

26. Ibid., xiii.

27. Astuto, et al. *Challenges to Dominant Assumptions Controlling Educational Reform*. Cited in Hord, *Professional Learning Communities*, 6.

bers, adults and students, are learners and that teachers and other community members are addressing challenges and issues, particularly those related to student learning."[28] "A group is a learning community when members share a common vision that learning is the primary purpose for their association and the ultimate value to preserve in their workplace and that learning outcomes are the primary criteria for evaluating the success of their work."[29] Scholars claim that we must insist that "if schools are to become real knowledge communities for all students, then teaching must be made into a real learning professionals for all teachers."[30] In fact, they claim that PLCs are those which seek to "enhance their effectiveness as professionals for the students' benefit . . . also termed as communities of continuous inquiry and improvement."[31] A PLC "is the identification and pursuit of explicit goals that foster the experimentation, results orientation, and commitment to continuous improvement that characterize the professional learning community."[32] PLCs operate under the assumption that the "core mission of formal education is not simply to ensure that students are taught but to ensure that they learn."[33] PLCs also function under the assumption that "educators . . . must work together to achieve their collective purpose of learning for all. Therefore, they create structures to promote a collaborative culture."[34] Finally, PLCs "judge their effectiveness on the basis of results."[35] The key idea here is that PLCs are guided by the core principles of learning, collaboration, and results. PLCs are defined by the challenges that educators face in developing them: developing and applying

28. Taylor, *Shaping the Culture of Learning Communities*, 1.
29. Huberman, *Can Start Teachers Create Learning Communities?*, 4.
30. Hargreaves, *Teaching in the Knowledge Society*, 161.
31. Hord, *Professional Learning Communities*, 6.
32. Dufour and Eaker, *Professional Learning Communities at Work*, 100.
33. Dufour, et al., *Recurring Themes of Professional Learning Communities*, 22.
34. Ibid., 36.
35. Ibid., 39.

shared knowledge; sustaining the hard work of change, and transforming school culture.

PLCs have six characteristics: (1) shared mission, vision, and values; (2) collective inquiry; (3) collaborative teams; (4) action orientation and experimentation; (5) continuous improvement; and (6) results orientation.[36] It has been documented that PLCs make a positive contribution to both staff and students in schools.[37] PLCs result in the reduction of isolation of teachers; increased commitment to the mission and goals of the school and increased vigor in working to strengthen the mission; shared responsibility for the total development of students and collective responsibility for students' success; powerful learning that defines good teaching and classroom practice, that creates new knowledge and beliefs about teaching and learners; increased meaning and understanding of the content that teachers teach and the roles that they play in helping all students achieve expectations; higher likelihood that teachers will be well informed, professionally renewed, and inspired to inspire students; more satisfaction and higher morale and lower rates of absenteeism; significant advances into making teaching adaptations for students and changes for learners made more quickly than in traditional schools; commitment to making significant and lasting changes; and higher likelihood of undertaking fundamental, systemic change. PLCs are also beneficial for students. It has also become evident that PLCs have the potential for benefiting students by decreasing dropout rates; lowering rates of absenteeism; increasing learning that is distributed more equitably in the smaller highschools, resulting in larger academic gains in math, science, history, and reading than in traditional schools; and decreasing achievement gaps between students from different backgrounds.

More specifically, various studies have documented the critical role of PLCs in ensuring teacher quality, student learning, and school improvement. A study of seventy-eight schools in eight districts in Tennessee specifically addressed the importance of

---

36. Dufour and Eaker, *Professional Learning Communities at Work*.
37. Hord, *Professional Learning Communities*.

collaboration and its relationship to continuous improvement.[38] This study classified school in three ways: "stuck," in-between," or "moving." Stuck schools had little or no concern for school-wide goals. Teachers worked in isolation with limited teacher learning and increasing degree of uncertainty about what and how to teach. Rosenholtz described stuck schools as schools where:

> Teachers seemed more concerned with their own identity than a sense of shared community. Teachers learned about the nature of their work randomly, not deliberately, tending to follow their individual instincts. Without shared governance, particularly in managing student conduct, the absolute number of students who claimed teachers' attention seemed greater . . . teachers talked of frustration, failure, tedium and managed to transfer those attributes to the students about whom they complained.[39]

Contrastingly, moving schools were characterized as being learning-enriched for both students and teachers. These schools had four characteristics: shared purpose and direction, teacher collaboration, teacher on-the-job learning, and teacher efficacy. Teacher commitment and student learning were evident in the "moving" schools.

> In the choreography of collaborative schools, norms of self-reliance appeared to be selfish infractions against the school community. With teaching defined as inherently difficult, many minds tended to work better than a few. Here, requests for and offers of advice and assistance seemed like moral imperatives and colleagues seldom acted without foresight and deliberate calculation. Teacher leaders reached out to others with encouragement, technical knowledge to solve classroom matters and enthusiasm for learning new things.[40]

---

38. Rosenholtz, *Teacher's Workplace*.
39. Ibid., 208.
40. Ibid.

This study concluded that "teachers who felt supported in their own ongoing learning and classroom practice were more committed and effective than those who did not. Support by means of teacher networks, cooperation among colleagues, and expanded professional roles increased teacher efficacy for meeting students' needs . . . teachers with a strong sense of their own efficacy were more likely to adopt new classroom behaviors and that a strong sense of efficacy encouraged teachers to stay in the profession."[41]

A study of the role of professional learning communities in sixteen highschools in California and Michigan provides ample evidence that a "collaborative community of practice in which teachers share instructional resources and reflections in practice appears essential to their persistence and success in innovating classroom practice."[42]

This study reported that there are three patterns of teaching practice, namely: (1) enacting traditions of practice (the teaching of traditional subjects and thus the learning of only traditional students); (2) the lowering of expectations and standards (the watering down of subjects when teachers encountered low-motivated students); and (3) attempting to innovate by engaging learners (in which subjects and teaching are considered dynamic in order to involve all students, which leads to greater learning by all). When teachers lower expectations, they tend to locate the problem in the students, whereas when innovating to engage students involved, teachers" move beyond or outside established frames for instruction to find or develop content and classroom strategies that will enable students to master core subject concepts."

These patterns had clear effects on the way autonomy was defined, perceived, and practiced in two highschool departments (English and Social Studies).

> In the Social Studies department, autonomy means isolation and reinforces the norms of individualism and conservativism. In the English department, professional

41. Hord, *Professional Learning Communities*, 10.

42. McLaughlin and Talbert, *Professional Communities and the Work of High School Teaching*, 22.

autonomy and strong community are mutually reinforcing, rather than oppositional. Here collegial support and interaction enable individual teachers to reconsider and revise their classroom practice confidently because department norms are mutually negotiated and understood.[43]

In addition, there were also striking differences in the motivation and career commitment of teachers. For example, these became very evident in two highschool departments (English and Social Studies).

> When teachers from the Oak Valley English and social studies departments told us how they feel about their job, it was hard to believe that they teach in the same school. Oak Valley English teachers of all pedagogical persuasions express pride in their department and pleasure in their workplace: "Not a day goes by that someone doesn't say how wonderful it is to work here," said one. In contrast, social studies teachers, weary of grappling alone with classrooms tensions, verbalize bitterness and professional disinvestment.[44]

Overall, this study found that highschools had strong and weak professional learning communities within and between school and departments respectively. Most highschools were reported to lack a strong culture of sharing and jointly-agreed practices. In this sense, one can conclude that weak communities were harmful for the students and the teachers. Comparatively, highschools that functioned with a strong culture of collaboration could have been positive or negative. In a positive sense, teachers can collaborate to challenge and expand each other's assumptions, ideas, and practice. In a negative sense, they can also collaborate to merely reinforce each others' false assumptions, bad habits, and ineffective practices.

A survey study of more than nine hundred teachers in twenty-four nationally selected restructuring elementary, middle, and

---

43. Ibid., 55.
44. Ibid., 82–83.

Large Scale Reforms

highschools documents highlighted the impact that professional communities can have on lasting change:

> A school-based professional community can offer support and motivation to teachers as they work to overcome the tight resources, isolation, time constraints and other obstacles they commonly encounter in today's schools. Within a strong professional community, for example, teachers can work collectively to set and enforce standards of instruction and learning. Instead of obeying bureaucratic rules, faculty members act according to teachers' norms of professional behavior and duty, which have been shown to be far stronger social control mechanisms. This also creates room within the school structure for principled disagreement and discussion on different issues, which can add to teachers' professional growth. In schools where professional community is strong, teachers work together more effectively, and put more effort into creating and sustaining opportunities for student learning. There must be support within the school for teachers who want to take risks and try new techniques and ideas. Otherwise, serious and lasting change cannot be sustained.[45]

This study concludes that professional communities are strong when they are guided by certain critical elements as well as when their certain structural conditions and social and human resources are met. Critical elements include reflective dialogue, de-privatization of practice, collective focus on student learning, collaboration, and shared norms and values. Structural conditions include time to meet and talk, physical proximity, communication structures, teacher empowerment and school autonomy. Social and human resources that appear to enhance professional communities include openness to improvement, trust and respect, cognitive and skills bases, supportive leadership, and socialization.

These three studies underscore the critical importance and necessity of professional learning communities and their connection to quality teaching and improved academic achievement for

---

45. Kruse, et al., *Building Professional Community in Schools*, 4.

all students. PLCs can serve as the mechanism to accomplish large scale reform.

Nonetheless, the concept of learning organizations and PLCs is very difficult to establish during large-scale education efforts and very hard to be sustained in the face of standardized reform. This is especially the case at the secondary level because of departmentalization and even balkanization of teachers' secondary-school subject communities.[46] One study of three innovative schools demonstrated that although the implementation of these concepts helps prevent schools from retreating to conventional processes, it paves the way for them to return to conventional patterns.[47] This project examined teacher and administrator perceptions of change over time in a variety of suburban and urban settings. Hargreaves and Goodson's report focuses on three innovative secondary schools that were studied as part of an eight-school international research project in Ontario, Canada, and in New York State. The key question of this study was whether these self-consciously created and established learning organizations and professional learning communities can "sustain their early promise of success in the face of predictable cycle of the 'attrition of change'; of pressure and envy in the surrounding district, profession and community; and of the historically specific and recent pressure of standardized reform."[48] Conclusions show that schools as learning organizations and professional learning communities were able to offset two of these three forces of change mentioned above. Schools were able to "renewe their teacher cultures, distributing leadership and planning for leadership succession,"[49] and be able to "manage their foreign relations with the community, other schools, and the district by curbing their arrogance, involving the community in decision making, and resisting the temptation to ask for too many favors from the district."[50] However, the greatest impediment was

46. Hargreaves, *Teaching in the Knowledge Society*.
47. Hargreaves and Goodson, *Educational Change Over Time*.
48. Ibid., 124.
49. Ibid., 152.
50. Ibid.

the standardized reform agenda. It undermined the knowledge of society-oriented schools and particularly the efforts of teachers.

The question then is to what extent schools can embrace the concept of PLCs in order to subvert and survive the pressures of standardization. Scholars described the irony of PLCs in the current educational climate as well as its future:

> The paradox of learning organizations and communities in education is that they are being advocated most strongly just at the point when standardized reform movements legislate the content and micromanage the process of learning to such a degree that there is little scope for teachers to learn in what little is left over. Professional learning communities are postmodern organizational forms struggling to survive in a modernistic, micromanaged and politicized educational world. Where standardized reform practices continue to tighten their grip, as is now the case in North America, the future for schools as learning organizations and professional learning communities that will develop the creativity and flexibility needed in the new knowledge economy does not look promising.[51]

This chapter reinforces the argument that there is explicit evidence of a relationship between PLCs and school improvement and student performance. Besides, there is also evidence that intentional pursuits of PLCs as capacity-building professional strategies and school cultures offer great promise for student achievement results. However, PLCs can be powerfully positive and/or negative[52] and are difficult and hard to establish given the conflictive and pervasive reality of standardized reform.[53]

Seven versions of PLCs have been identified and analyzed.[54] These include communities of containment and control (the titular community, the totalitarian training sect, the autistic surveil-

---

51. Ibid., 153.
52. Hargreaves, *Leading Professional Learning Communities*.
53. McNeil, *Contradictions of School Reform*.
54. Hargreaves, *Leading Professional Learning Communities*.

lance system, and the speed dating agency) and communities of empowerment (the living and learning community, the inclusive and responsive community, and the activist and empowered community). The point here is to highlight that just like any other educational effort and/or concept, PLCs should be critically reexamined and revised. Its original and noble principles and intentions can be distorted. It is critical and essential to revisit what and how they are functioning so as to avoid having them "amount to a corruption of their fundamental principles and purposes—being little more than a change in title, a hyperactive diversion, an autistic obsession with numbers and targets, or a pretext for insisting on compliance and imposing control."[55] In light of the advent of large-scale reforms and the emerging importance of leadership as well as PLCs as concepts and mechanisms that can facilitate its embedding and deepening, what and how does Fullan assesses this period?

Michael Fullan's Assessment of Large-Scale Reform, Leadership, and Professional Learning Communities

In terms of large-scale reform, the purpose of school reform, its main enemies, and the need for capacity-building and sustainability at the three levels (school, district and state) are clearly identified. Likewise, the critical role of the principal is emphasized as well as a framework for leadership in a culture of change is suggested with comments on its significant relationship to student learning. Finally, the importance of relationships is deemed critical and the place of PLCs in a larger perspective (a system quality) is also considered. While acknowledging that PLCs are difficult to establish, they should be rooted and guided by dignity and respect and should not be treated as the implementation of another innovation. It is not about PLCs but about professional learning which

---

55. Ibid., 22.

Large Scale Reforms

will lead to system transformation. Let us briefly review his major points.

The "primary purpose of school reform is not to adopt or even internalize a valuable external model. The primary goal is to alter the capacity of the school to engage in improvement"[56] through working with whole systems. This calls for both an accountability pillar and a capacity-building pillar.

Educators face tensions and dilemmas, and therefore it is critical to make a distinction between the forces for accountability and capacity-building. The main enemies of large-scale reform are overload and extreme fragmentation. The reasons large-scale reforms have failed is that there is a lack of understanding "that both local school development and the quality of the surrounding infrastructure are critical for lasting success."[57] The "inside story" refers to the internal dynamics of school change. The key here is to focus on reculturing in addition to restructuring. The "inside-outside" story highlights the external forces that impact schools. The point here is that schools cannot do it alone and the implication is that teachers and principals must reframe their roles in relationship to the outside environment. The "outside-in" story refers to the agencies that are external to the school. The key here is that effective schools collaborate with powerful external forces such as parents and community, technology, corporate connections, government policy, and the wider teaching profession.[58]

Sustainability is crucial for large-scale reform. After underscoring the resurgence of large-scale reform and briefly reviewing the failure of previous educational reform attempts, particularly in the US, eight factors are listed as crucial not only for its establishment but most importantly for its sustainability. The system context should be upgraded. "No large-scale reform will happen or be sustained in the absence of a strong teaching profession and corresponding infrastructure."[59] Coherence is the main task. In order

---

56. Fullan, *Whole School Reform*, 5.
57. Fullan, *The Three Stories of Education Reform*, 2.
58. Hargreaves and Fullan, *What's Worth Fighting for Out There?*
59. Fullan, *The Return of Large-Scale Reform*, 21.

to be effective, schools and schools systems need to be selective, integrative, and focused. "Large-scale reform will require units to make connections and synergized activities around common priorities."[60] There is also a need for the establishment of cross-over structures. These are "the variety of agencies, offices, and institutions that play a role in implementation."[61] The primary issue here is "to conceive of initial implementation structures as mobilizing commitment and capacity (will and skill, if you like)."[62] Allocate resources to increase the capacity of people to make improvements (downward investment/upward identity). Invest in quality materials. "To achieve large-scale reform you cannot depend on people's capacity to bring about substantial change in the short run, so you need to propel the process with high quality teaching and training materials (print, video, electronic)."[63] Integrate pressure and support. Lateral accountability as well as support is critical. Educators need to get out of implementing someone else's agenda. Reform will never occur on a large scale until teachers and others get out of the mindset that they are always implementing someone else's reform agenda and that they must "practice the 'positive politics' of defining their own legitimate reform agenda in the context of state policy."[64] Finally, educators are advised to work with systems, which means "conceptualizing strategies with whole systems in mind" not to work with schools in isolation but to "figure out how to work with the district as a system" and not to "focus on state policy as autonomous components, but work at alignment and connections."[65]

The key to large scale reform is to establish and develop capacity-building and accountability at three levels: the schools, the district, and the state. At the school level, what is needed is school capacity, namely: teachers' knowledge, skills and dispositions,

60. Ibid., 21.
61. Ibid., 22.
62. Ibid., 22.
63. Ibid., 23.
64. Ibid., 25.
65. Ibid., 25.

professional community, program coherence, technical resources, and principal leadership.[66] School capacity is slow to come and be attained due to difficulties in parents' and communities' participation, assessment literacy efforts, resources, staff turnover, the reconciling of district initiatives, and sustaining success. At the district level, improving implies that the "infrastructure counts. It can lead the way or it can actually undercut efforts of individual schools on the move, while neglecting other schools that are persistently failing."[67] Moreover, the success of large-scale systemic improvement for districts depends on multiple factors, namely: compelling conceptualization; collective moral purpose; the right bus; capacity building; lateral capacity building; ongoing learning; productive learning; a demanding culture; external partners; and focused financial investments.[68]

Finally, at the state level, the key is to implement a mixture of both pressure and support strategies. This refers to both a specific and generic infrastructure. Using the description and analysis of England's National Literacy and Numeracy Strategy, specific infrastructure refers to the literacy and numeracy components and their main implementation elements. Generic infrastructure refers to the "policies related to the overall quality of the teaching profession."[69] "Policy makers need to turn their attention to developing capacities and interactions across the three levels."[70] There is a need for "a set of policies on accountability and capacity-building" that will "take into account all three levels and their interrelationships,"[71] acknowledge the "limitations of a tightly orchestrated tri-level strategy, be aware of the "quality, morale and internal commitment of the teaching profession qua profession,"[72]

66. Newmann, et al., *Successful School Restructuring*.
67. Fullan, *The Return of Large-Scale Reform*, 16.
68. Fullan, *Leadership Across the System*, 43–44.
69. Barber, *High Expectations and Standards*; Barber, *Large Scale Reform in England*; Barber, *Accountability vs. Autonomy. Education*
70. Fullan, *The Return of Large-Scale Reform*, 21.
71. Ibid., 21.
72. Ibid., 22.

broaden "the curriculum beyond literacy and numeracy,"[73] and understand that "change in complex society will never be linear."[74]

In addition to acknowledging the return of large-scale reform, its enemies, and suggesting that it takes place at the school, district and state levels with sustainability as the goal, leadership ,and professional learning communities are crucial factors.[75] The importance of leadership in education reform has been documented at length.[76] More specifically, the role of system leadership is cited as a necessary ingredient and crucial variable for large-scale reform. The importance of leadership has been captured by the role of the principal and his relationship to student learning.

In an era of large-scale reform, the work of the principal has become increasingly complex and constrained. Simply stated, principals have become too dependent on context. "Dependency is created by two interrelated conditions: overload and corresponding vulnerability to packaged solutions."[77] Principals find themselves receiving and responding to multiple,fragmented, and incoherent innovations. As a consequence, it is understandable and expected that they may feel tempted by and vulnerable to the latest recipe for success that appears. This advice could be damaging and

73. Ibid., 23
74. Ibid., 23.

75. Fullan, *Leading in a Culture of Change*; Fullan, *Leadership Across the System*; Fullan, *Turnaround Leadership*; Fullan, *The Moral Imperative of School Leadership*; Fullan, *Professional Learning Communities Write Large*; Fullan, *The New Meaning of Educational Change*; Leithwood, et al., *Strategic Leadership for Large-Scale Reform*.

76. Bolman and Deal, *Reframing Organizations*; Elmore, *Building a New Structure for School Leadership*; Fink and Resnick, *Developing Principals As Instructional Leaders*; Hargreaves and Fink, *Sustainable Leadership*; Hord, *Professional Learning Communities*; Leithwood, et al., *Large Scale Reform*; Leithwood, *Strategic Leadership for Large Scale Reform*; Marzano, et al., *School Leadership That Works*; Méndez-Morse, *Leadership Characteristics That Facilitate School Change*; Resnick and Glennan, *Leadership for Learning*; Senge, *Leading Learning Organizations*; Sergiovanni, *Leadership*; Sergiovanni, *The Lifeworld of Leadership*; Spillane, et al., *Investigating School Leadership Practice*; Stoll and Fink, *It's About Learning (and It's About Time)*; Waters, et al., *Balanced Leadership*.

77. Fullan, *Leadership for the 21st Century*, 6.

deceiving. There is "no definite answer to the 'how' question."[78] Instead, principals are encouraged to give up the search for the silver bullet in order to overcome dependency.

Principals are also encouraged to learn from resistance and dissonance; to advocate for community reform and become assessment-literate; to manage emotionally; and to be hopeful by fighting for lost causes. The future and coming challenge in the minds of policy-makers is to scale up. For this, it is necessary to realize that educational leaders of the twenty-first century should "look for answers close at hand and reaching out, knowing that there is no clear solution."[79]

The role of leadership in large-scale reform as the key driver is also underscored.

> Leadership is to this decade what standards were to the 1990s, if you want large-scale, sustainable reform. You can get some improvement by tightening standards, but only to a point, as we have seen in England. In order to get deeper, you have to capture the energy, ideas, and commitment of teachers and principals. It takes leadership—a certain kind of leadership—to do this.[80]

This assertion is based on the argument that effective leaders create energizing environments. Particularly important here is the evidence gathered after examination of leadership cases in business and education.[81] The commonality of leaderships across these sectors is that learning organizations in complex times are characterized by moral purpose, an understanding of the change process, strong relationships, knowledge-sharing capacities, and coherence- and connectedness-making abilities. These are the components of the framework that should guide principals that lead in a culture of change.

Besides leadership for learning organizations, a four-year evaluation report of England's NLNS underscores that "strategic"

78. Ibid., 8.
79. Ibid., 10.
80. Fullan, *Leadership Across the System*, 16.
81. Fullan, *Leading in a Culture of Change*.

and "distributed" forms of leadership are critical for large-scale initiatives.[82] Evidence clearly shows that strategic leadership is "widely distributed and enacted; it has the flexibility to mature over time from relatively simple additive forms to more holistic forms in which relationships within and across levels of leadership become highly interactive."[83] The point here is to question and debunk the three assumptions prevalent in contemporary leadership literature. These refer to the assumption that "leadership needs to be transactional and managerial in nature"[84] when driving large-scale reform, that "transformational leadership is typically, if not necessarily, provided by talented leaders,"[85] and that "distributed and hierarchical forms of leadership are somehow incompatible and that distributed forms are superior."[86] The point here is that there is a need for a greater and more complex orientation and application to leadership "than much of the literature would suggest and one that seems prone to exaggerated claims rooted in democratic ideology."[87]

Finally, in terms of leadership, the significant relationship of the principal to student learning is highlighted.[88] The key to success is the school principal.[89] The principal is the nerve centre of school improvement. When principal leadership is strong, even the most challenged schools thrive. When it is weak, schools fail or badly underperform."[90]

The principalship is not improving because of individual, collective, and more importantly systemic reasons. The key to improving the principalship is to get inside the black box of success, to identify the barriers that block this sustained success and

82. Leithwood, et al., *Strategic Leadership for Large-Scale Reform.*
83. Ibid., 75.
84. Ibid.
85. Ibid.
86. Ibid.
87. Ibid., 76.
88. Fullan, *Turnaround Leadership.*
89. Fullan, *Quality Leadership-Quality Learning.*
90. Ibid., 1.

to how to go forward. The recommendations here are to raise the bar for the principalship, to improve the conditions under which they work, and to challenge those who are not performing well. The goal here is to "dramatically increase leadership across the system."[91]

In addition to highlighting the importance of leadership, relationships are critical. "Development of individuals is not sufficient. New relationships (as found in a professional learning community) are crucial, but only if they work at the hard task of establishing greater program coherence and the addition of resources."[92] Dignity and respect must be at the core of these relationships and at the formation of PLCs. These should function as a source of motivation. It is about a socially based solution where teachers come together to reflect and collaborate on the ethical and moral dimensions of their work. "Fostering PLCs should include forums for teachers to collectively reflect on and collaborate on the ethical and moral dimensions of their work and behavior."[93] In addition to the individualistic bias and ethical implications of PLCs, these "should not be confined to latest ideas and innovations. They should not be places for well-meaning superficial exchanges."[94] The depth of PLCs requires consistent reflection and problem-solving. PLCs are not merely intra-school isolated phenomenon. It is about the fostering of collaborative cultures across districts, cross-school learning, or lateral capacity building. In sum, intra- as well as inter-school learning is needed for system transformation. In this sense, Fullan approachs PLCs as a capacity-building strategy that takes hard work because of an institutional culture that does not connect well to other levels of the system.

Nonetheless, PLCs are difficult to establish. A lack of focus and investment on the part of policy-makers and the comfort of privatization in teaching practices are some of the reasons for this. PLCs "are not making their way with any substance and continuity

91. Ibid., 18–19.
92. Fullan, *Leading in a Culture of Change*.
93. Fullan, *The New Meaning of Educational Change*, 50.
94. Ibid.

inside the classroom."[95] Getting at the core of improving instructional practice and changing norms of autonomy and loyalty is hard and complex.[96] The answer is "deep engagement with their colleagues and with mentors in exploring, refining, and improving their practice as well as setting up an environment in which this not only can happen but is encouraged, rewarded, and pressed to happen."[97] The real challenge here is to change the prevailing culture of administration and teaching in schools. The danger of current reform strategies is the dramatic expectation of a turnaround of a failing schools. These strategies are narrowly conceived, under conceptualized, "too little and too late, work on only a small part of the problem, and unwittingly establish conditions that actually guarantee unsustainability."[98] In this sense, Fullan's approach to PLCs sounds like an implementation strategy. Its results may be superficial, narrowly conceived, and therefore temporary as he forcefully documents in the turnaround school phenomenon.

The real challenge then for PLCs is to place them in a larger, systemic perspective. The argument is that "if we do not examine and improve the overall system at three levels, we will never have more than temporary havens of excellence that come and go. Without attention to the larger system, professional learning communities will always be in the minority, never rising above 20% in popularity in the nation, and will not last beyond the tenure of those fortunate enough to have established temporary collaborative cultures."[99] The solution lies in the tri-level strategy that builds capacity across the three levels: school, district, and state. This implies the need to address the problem of bias toward individualistic solutions; the radical need for systems thinkers in action; the importance of learning from each other as we go and the danger of waiting for others to act. This is about "changing cultures

95. Ibid., 56.
96. Campbell, *Challenges in Fostering Ethical Knowledge*; Elmore, *The Hollow Core of Leadership*; Elmore, *School Reform from the Inside Out*.
97. Fullan, *The New Meaning of Educational Change*, 57.
98. Ibid., 20.
99. Fullan, *Leadership and Sustainability*, 210.

Large Scale Reforms

to create new contexts."[100] This is also the key to sustainability.[101] Sustainability is about changing and developing the social environment. "Professional learning communities at large are not about the proliferation of single schools; they are about creating new environments across the system through tri-level development."[102]

Linking large scale reforms to professional learning communities is the moral imperative of leadership and breakthrough system transformation. The principal is strategically placed best to accomplish the moral imperative of schools.[103] "Leading schools requires principals with the courage and capacity to build new cultures based on trusting relationships and a culture of disciplined inquiry and action."[104] These new cultures should be built not only at the individual and school but also at the regional and societal level for large scale system transformation to occur. On the other hand, it is essential to consider the starting point and continuum of development of schools development principals find themselves in. Principals should be able to recognize the instructional continuum their particular schools are at. The distinction between performance training sects and professional learning communities is a good starting point.[105]

However, whereas earlier PLCs grounded on informed prescription[106] are appropriate for schools and districts that have low leader capacity, unprepared teachers, and poor performance, later characterization of PLCs as performance training sects as "crude" are criticized, putting advocates of prescription on the defensive without giving them any convincing reasons to question their approaches, giving it gives license to professional learning communities without any detailed strategy for accomplishing change

100. Ibid., 218.
101. Hargreaves and Fink, *Sustainable Leadership*.
102. Fullan, *Leadership and Sustainability*, 219.
103. Fullan, *The Moral Imperative of School Leadership*.
104. Ibid., 45.
105. Hargreaves, *Teaching in the Knowledge Society*.
106. Fullan, *The Moral Imperative of School Leadership*.

in classrooms on a large scale.[107] The problem is that these descriptions do not deal with instructional transformation. Instead of granting the assumption that greater precision implies greater precision, what is needed is a strategy of breakthrough system through personalization, precision, and professional learning. At the center of this breakthrough is moral purpose. Moral purpose in large scale reforms demands the reconceptualization and transformation of leadership in school systems. Moral purpose in the creation, building, nurturing, and sustaining of professional learning communities in the midst of an increasing standardized reform era is not only about individual but also organizational development.

To recap, the arrival, reality, need, and complexity of large-scale reform is acknowledged. Overload and fragmentation are its main enemies. Its solution is coherence through a redefined and reframed social- and action-based systemic application of leadership and professional learning. Capacity-building and sustainability efforts are at the core of this equation. Professional learning communities can help accomplish large-scale reform. Moral purpose demands a reconceptualization of leadership and a clear realization of the continuum from individual to organizational development. In a nutshell, it is about integrating individual and organizational development.

A Final Word

This book describes four historical movements of efforts to change and better schools. I have attempted to describe its origins, major proponents, and practical implications for educational reform and theory. I have also explored and examined the observations and commentaries of noted scholar Fullan in an attempt to describe how he contributes to the past, present, and future dialogue on school reform and educational change.

107. Fullan, et al., *Breakthrough*; Hargreaves, *Teaching in the Knowledge Society*.

Large Scale Reforms

As has been seen throughout this book, Fullan's scholarly commentary never led a change period but rather provided a perspective of why certain initiatives (within the period) succeeded and others did not. At the end of the innovation and diffusion period, Fullan acknowledged the rational and linear nature and process of educational reform as well as the absence of a clear and articulate theory of action which implied that adoption equated implementation. In the middle of the following period, Fullan presented himself as an advocate for school improvement in addition to school effectiveness. Fullan argued in favor of the importance of process factors in addition to outcomes. In both the middle and at the end of the school restructuring and reculturing movements, Fullan acknowledges and comments on the existence, value, and necessity of restructuring; however, he claims that school improvement is not likely if there is no space for teachers and principals to question their beliefs as well as the values and norms that shape and guide their relationships. In Fullan's terms, reculturing requires attention to the culture of the schools as it affects its teaching and leadership force. Perhaps the exception to being in the middle and at the end of the previous movements is Fullan's participation in the current large-scale reform period. His most recent work and involvement as a consultant and project evaluator with countries and states (i.e., England, Ontario) may represent an attempt to lead the change period (large-scale reform). Fullan briefly acknowledges the arrival, reality, need, and complexity of large-scale reform as well as its main enemies, namely, overload and fragmentation, and his advocacy for capacity-building and sustainability.

Bibliography for Innovation and Diffusion Period

Berman, P., and Milbrey W. McLaughlin. *Federal Programs Supporting Educational Change: Volume VIII. Implementing and Sustaining Innovations.* Santa Monica: The RAND Corporation, R-1589/8-HEW, 1978.

Berman, Paul. "Three Perspectives on Innovation: Technological, Political, and Cultural." In *Improving Schools: Using What we Know,* 17–41. Beverly Hills: Sage, 1981.

Coleman, James S., et al. *Equality of Educational Opportunity.* Washington: National Center for Educational Statistics, 1966.

Datnow, Amanda, et al., *Extending Educational Reform: From One School to Many.* New York: Routledge/Falmer, 2002.

Datnow, Amanda. "Gender Politics in School Reform." In *The Sharp Edge of Educational Change: Teaching, Leading and The Realities of Reform,* 131–155. New York: Routledge/Falmer, 2002,

David, Jane L. "What It Takes to Restructure Education." *Educational Leadership 48* (1991): 11–15.

Edmonds, Ronald. "Effective Schools for the Urban Poor." *Educational Leadership 37* (1979): 15–27.

Elmore, Richard F. "On Changing the Structure of Public Schools." In *Restructuring Schools: The Next Generation of Education Reform,* 1–28. San Francisco: Jossey-Bass, 1990.

———, and Deanna Burney. "School Variation and Systemic Instructional Component in Community School District #2, New York City."

———, et al. *Restructuring in the Classroom: Teaching, Learning, and School Organization.* San Francisco: Jossey-Bass, 1996.

Fink, Dean. "The Attrition of Educational Change over Time: The Case of Innovative, Model, Lighthouse Schools." In *The Sharp Edge of Educational Change: Teaching, Leading and the Realities of Reform,* 29–51. New York: Routledge and Falmer, 2000.

Bibliography for Innovation and Diffusion Period

———. "The Law of Unintended Consequences: The 'Real' Cost of Top-Down Reform." *Journal of Educational Change* 4 (2003): 105–28.

———, and Louise Stoll. "Educational Change: Easier Said Than Done." In *International Handbook of Educational Change.* Edited by Andy Hargreaves, et al., 297–321. The Netherlands: Kluwer Academic, 1998.

Fuhrman, Susan H., et al. "School Reform in the United States: Putting It into Context." In *Reforming Education.* dited by Jacobson, Stephen L., and Robert Berne, 3–27. Thousand Oaks, CA: Corwin, 1993.

Fullan, Michael. *Change Forces: Probing the Depths of Educational Reform.* London: Falmer, 1993.

———. *Change Forces: The Sequel.* Bristol, PA: Falmer, 1999.

———. *Change Forces with a Vengeance.* London: RoutledgeFalmer, 2003.

———. *Leadership and Sustainability: System Thinkers in Action.* Thousand Oaks, CA: Corwin, 2005.

———. *Leading in a Culture of Change.* San Francisco: Jossey-Bass, 2001.

———. "Overview of the Innovative Process and the User." *Interchange* 3 (1972): 1–46.

———, and Alan Pomfret. "Research on Curriculum and Instruction Implementation." *Review of Educational Research* 47 (1977): 335–97.

———. "The Meaning of Educational Change: A Quarter of a Century of Learning." In *International Handbook of Educational Change.* Edited by Andy Hargreaves, et al., 214–28. The Netherlands: Kluwer Academic, 1998.

———. *The Moral Imperative of School Leadership.* Thousand Oaks, CA: Corwin, 2003.

———. *The New Meaning of Educational Change.* 1st ed. New York: Teachers College Press, 1982.

———. *The New Meaning of Educational Change.* 2nd ed. New York: Teachers College Press, 1991.

———. "The Return of Large-Scale Reform." *Journal of Educational Change* 1 (2000): 5–28.

Goodlad, John, et al. *Behind the Classroom Door.* Worthington, OH: Charles A. Jones, 1970.

Gross, Neal, et al. *Implementing Organizational Innovations: A Sociological Analysis of Planned Educational Change.* New York: Basic, 1971.

Hargreaves, Andy. *Changing Teachers, Changing Times: Teachers' Work and Culture in the Postmodern Age.* New York: Teachers College Press, 1994.

———. "Educational Change Over Time? The Sustainability and Nonsustainability of Three Decades of Secondary School Change and Continuity." *Educational Administration Quarterly* 42 (2006:) 3–41.

———. "The Emotions of Educational Change." In *International Handbook of Educational Change.* Edited by Andy Hargreaves, et. al., 558–75. The Netherlands: Kluwer Academic, 1998.

———. "The Emotional Geographies of Teaching." *Teachers' College Record* 103 (2001): 1056–80.

Bibliography for Innovation and Diffusion Period

———. *Teaching in the Knowledge Society: Education in the Age of Insecurity.* New York: Teachers College Press, 2003.

———, et al. "Introduction." In *International Handbook of Educational Change.* Edited by Andy Hargreaves, et al., 1–7. The Netherlands: Kluwer Academic, 1998.

Havelock, Ronald G. *The Change Agent's Guide to Innovation in Education.* Englewood Cliffs, NJ: Educational Technology Publications, 1973.

Hopkins, David, et al. *School Improvement in an Era of Change.* New York: Teachers College Press, 1994.

House, Ernest. "Technology Versus Craft." *Curriculum Studies 11* (1979): 1–15.

Huberman, A.M., and Matthew B. Miles. *Innovations Up Close.* New York: Plenum, 1984.

Jensen, A.R. "How Much Can We Boost IQ and Scholastic Achievement?" *Harvard Educational Review 39* (1969): 1–123.

Lieberman, Ann. "The Growth of Educational Change As a Field of Study: Understanding Its Roots and Branches." In *International Handbook of Educational Change.* Edited by Andy Hargreaves, et al., 13–20. The Netherlands: Kluwer Academic, 1998.

Louis, K.S., and Matthew B. Miles. *Improving the Urban High School: What Works and Why.* New York: Teachers College Press, 1990.

Murphy, Joseph. "The Educational Reform Movement of the 1980's: A Comprehensive Analysis." In *The Reform of American Public Education in the 1980's: Perspectives and Cases*, 3–55. Berkeley: McCutchan, 1990.

National Commission on Excellence in Education. "A Nation at Risk: The Imperative of Educational Reform."

Oakes, Jeannie, et al. *Becoming Good American Schools: The Struggle for Civic Virtue in Education Reform.* San Francisco: Jossey-Bass, 2000.

Peterson, Penelope L., et al. "Learning from School Restructuring." *American Educational Research Journal 33* (1996): 119–53.

Rogers, Everett M. *Diffusion of Innovations.* New York: Free, 1983.

Sarason, Seymour B. *Barometers of Change: Individual, Institutional and Social Transformation.* San Francisco: Jossey-Bass, 1996.

———. *The Culture of the School and the Problem of Change.* Boston: Allyn and Bacon, 1971.

———. *The Predictable Failure of Educational Reform: Can We Change Course Before It's Too Late?* San Francisco: Jossey-Bass, 1991.

———. "World War II and Schools." In *International Handbook of Educational Change.* Edited by Andy Hargreaves, et al., 23–26. The Netherlands: Kluwer Academic, 1998.

Smith, L.M., and Pat M. *Anatomy of Educational Innovation.* New York: Wiley, 1971.

Smith, M.S., and Jennifer A. O'Day. "Systemic School Reform." In *The Politics of Curriculum and Testing: The 1990 Yearbook of the Politics of Education*, 233–67. Philadelphia: Falmer, 1991.

Bibliography for Innovation and Diffusion Period

Smylie, M.A., and George S. Perry. "Restructuring Schools for Improving Tomorrow." In *International Handbook of Educational Change*. Edited by Andy Hargreaves, et al., 976–1005. The Netherlands: Kluwer Academic, 1998.

Wohlstetter, Priscilla. "Getting School-Based Management Right: What Works and What Doesn't." In *The Challenge of School Change*, 181–90. Thousand Oaks, CA: Corwin, 1997.

Bibliography for School Effectiveness and School Improvement

Ainscow, Mel, et al. *School Improvement in an Era of Change: An Overview of the Improving the Quality of Education for All Project.* Paper presented at the annual meeting of the American Educational Research Association, New Orleans, 1994.

Berman, P., and Milbrey W. McLaughlin. *Federal Programs Supporting Educational Change: Volume VIII. Implementing and Sustaining Innovations.* Santa Monica: The RAND Corporation, R-1589/8-HEW, 1978.

Berman, Paul. "Three Perspectives on Innovation: Technological, Political, and Cultural." In *Improving Schools: Using What We Know*, 17–41. Beverly Hills, : Sage, 1981.

Bernstein, Basil. "Education Cannot Compensate for Society." *New Society 387* (1970): 344–47.

Bowles, S., and Herbert Gintis. *Schooling in Capitalist America.* New York: Basic, 1976

Caldwell, B., and Jim Spinks. *The Self-Managing School.* Lewes: Falmer, 1988.

Chubb, John E. "Why the Current Wave of School Reform Will Fail." *Public Interest 90* (1998): 28–49.

Clark, David L., et al. "Effective Schools and School Improvement: A Comprehensive Analysis of Two Lines of Inquiry." *Educational Administration Quarterly 20* (1984): 41–68.

Coleman, James S., et al. *Equality of Educational Opportunity.* Washington: National Center for Educational Statistics, 1966.

Crandall, David, et al., *People, Policies and Practice. Examining the Chain of School Improvement.* Volumes 1–10. Andover, MA: The Network, 1982.

Creemers, B. P. M., and Gerry J. Reezigt. "School Effectiveness and School Improvement: Sustaining Links." *School Effectiveness and School Improvement 8* (1997): 396–429.

Edmonds, Richard F. "Effective Schools for the Urban Poor." *Educational Leadership 37* (1979): 15–27.

Bibliography for School Effectiveness and School Improvement

Elmore, Richard F. "Getting to Scale With Good Education Practice." *Harvard Educational Review* 66 (1996): 1–26.

———. "Reform and Culture of Authority in Schools. *Educational Administration Quarterly* 23 (1987): 60–78.

Fink, D., and Louise Stoll. "Educational Change: Easier Said Than Done." In *International Handbook of Educational Change*. Edited by Andy Hargreaves, et al., 297–321. The Netherlands: Kluwer Academic, 1998.

Fullan, Michael. "Change Processes and Strategies at the Local Level." *Elementary School Journal* 85 (1985): 391–420.

———. "Overview of the Innovative Process and the User." *Interchange* 3 (1972): 1–46.

———. *The New Meaning of Educational Change*. 2nd ed. New York: Teachers College Press, 1991.

———. *What's Worth Fighting for in Your School?* Milton Keynes: Open University Press, 1992.

Gray, John, et al. *Merging Traditions: The Future of Research on School Effectiveness and School Improvement*. New York: Cassell, 1996,

Hargreaves, A. *Changing Teachers, Changing Times: Teachers' Work and Culture in the Postmodern Age*. New York: Teachers College Press, 1994

———, and Michael Fullan, eds. *Change Wars*. Bloomington: Solution Tree, 2008.

Hargreaves, David. "School Culture, School Effectiveness and School Improvement." *School Effectiveness and School Improvement* 6 (1995): 23–46.

Hopkins, David. *School Improvement for Real*. New York: Routledge Falmer, 2001.

———, et al. *Improving the Quality of Education for All*. London: David Fulton, 1996.

———, et al. *School Improvement in an Era of Change*. New York: Teachers College Press, 2001.

House, Ernest R. "Three Perspectives on Innovation." In *Improving Schools: Using What We Know*. Beverly Hills: Sage, 1981.

Huberman, A.M., and Matthew B. Miles. *Innovations Up Close*. New York: Plenum, 1984.

Jacobson, S.J., and James A. Conway. *Educational Leadership in an Age of Reform*. New York: Longman, 1990.

Joyce, Bruce R. "The Doors to School Improvement." *Educational Leadership* 48 (1991): 59–62.

Levine, D.U., and Lawrence Lezotte, L. W. *Unusually Effective Schools: A Review and Analysis of Research and Practice*. Madison: National Center for Effective Schools Research and Development, 1990.

Lezotte, Lawrence W. "Base School Improvement on What We Know about Effective Schools." *American School Board Journal* 176 (1989): 18–20.

Lieberman, Ann. "The Growth of Educational Change As a Field of Study: Understanding Its Roots and Branches." In *International Handbook*

Bibliography for School Effectiveness and School Improvement

of *Educational Change.* Edited by Andy Hargreaves, et al., 13-20. The Netherlands: Kluwer Academic, 1998.

Little, Judith W. "The Persistence of Privacy: Autonomy and Initiative in Teachers' Professional Relations." *Teachers College Record 91* (1990): 509-36.

Louis, K.S., and Matthew B. Miles. *Improving the Urban High School: What Works and Why.* New York: Teachers College Press, 1990.

Louis, Karen S. "Beyond 'Managed Change': Rethinking How Schools Improve." *School Effectiveness and School Improvement 5* (1994): 2-25.

Mortimore, Peter. "The Vital Hours: Reflecting on Research on Schools and Their Effects." In *International Handbook of Educational Change.* dited by Andy Hargreaves, et al., 85-99. The Netherlands: Kluwer Academic, 1998.

———. *School Matters: The Junior Years.* Wells: Open, 1988.

Murphy, John. "School Effectiveness and School Restructuring: Contributions to Educational Improvement." *School Effectiveness and School Improvement 3* (1992): 90-109

Murphy, Joseph. "The Educational Reform Movement of the 1980's: A Comprehensive Analysis." In *The Reform of American Public Education in the 1980's: Perspectives and Cases*, 3-55. Berkeley: McCutchan, 1990.

Nuttall, Desmond L., et al. "Differential School Effectiveness." *International Journal of Educational Research 13* (1989): 769-76.

Plowden Report. *Children and Their Primary Schools.* London: HMSO, 1967.

Purkey, S.D., and Marshall S. Smith. "Effective Schools: A Review." *The Elementary School Journal 83* (1983): 427-52.

Rosenholtz, Susan. *Teacher's Workplace: The Social Organization of Schools.* New York: Longman, 1989.

Rutter, Michael., et al. *Fifteen Thousand Hours: Secondary Schools and Their Effects on Children.* London: Open, 1979.

Reynolds, David, et al. "Linking School Effectiveness Knowledge and School Improvement Practice: Towards a Synergy." *School Effectiveness and School Improvement 4* (1993): 37-58.

Rogers, Everett M. *Diffusion of Innovations.* New York: Free, 1983.

Sammons, Pamela, et al. *Key Characteristics of Effective Schools: A Review of School Effectiveness Research.* London: OFSTED, 1995.

Sarason, Seymour B. *The Culture of the School and the Problem of Change.* Boston: Allyn and Bacon, 1971.

Scheerens, Jaap. *Effective Schooling: Research, Theory and Practice.* London: Cassell, 1992.

Sirotnik, Kenneth A. "Ecological Images of Change: Limits and Possibilities." In *International Handbook of Educational Change.* dited by Andy Hargreaves, et al., 181-97. The Netherlands: Kluwer Academic, 1998.

Stoll, Loiuse. "Linking School Effectiveness and School Improvement: Issues and Possibilities." In *Merging Traditions: The Future of Research on School Effectiveness and School Improvement*, 51-73. New York: Cassell, 1996.

———, and Dean Fink. "School Effectiveness and School Improvement: Voices from the Field." *School Effectiveness and School Improvement* 5 (1994): 149–77.

Teddlie, C., and Sam Stringfield. *Schools Make a Difference: Lessons Learned from a Ten-year Study of School Effects.* New York: Teachers College Press, 1993.

Van Velzen, W.G., et al. *Making School Improvement Work: A Conceptual Guide to Practice.* Leuven, Belgium: ACCO, 1985.

Bibliography for School Restructuring and Reculturing

Barth, Roland S. "The Culture Builder." *Educational Leadership* 59 (2002): 7–11.

Berends, M., and Bruce King. "A Description of Restructuring in Nationally Nominated Schools: Legacy of the Iron Cage?" *Educational Policy* 8 (1994): 28–50.

Bolman, L.G., and Terrence Deal. *Reframing Organizations: Artistry, Choice and Leadership*, 4th ed. San Francisco: Jossey-Bass, 2008.

Carnegie Forum on Education and the Economy. *A Nation Prepared: Teachers for the 21st Century*. Report of the Carnegie Task Force on Teaching as a Profession. Washington: Carnegie Forum, 1996.

Cuban L., and David Tyack. *Tinkering Toward Utopia: A Century of Public School Reform*. Cambridge: Harvard University Press, 1992.

Datnow, Amanda, et al., *Extending Educational Reform: From One School to Many*. New York: Routledge/Falmer, 2002.

David, Jane L. "What It Takes to Restructure Education." *Educational Leadership* 48 (1991): 11–15.

Deal, T.D., and Kent D. Peterson. *Shaping School Culture: The Heart of Leadership*. San Francisco: Jossey-Bass, 1985.

Elmore, Richard F. "Getting to Scale with Good Education Practice." *Harvard Educational Review* 66 (1996): 1–26.

———. *Restructuring Schools: The Next Generation of Educational Reform*. San Francisco: Jossey-Bass, 1990.

———. "On Changing the Structure of Public Schools." In *Restructuring Schools: The Next Generation of Education Reform*, 1–28. San Francisco: Jossey-Bass.

———, and Deanna Burney. "School Variation and Systemic Instructional Component in Community School District #2, New York City." University of Pennsylvania, Consortium for Policy Research in Education.

———, et al. *Restructuring in the Classroom: Teaching, Learning, and School Organization*. San Francisco: Jossey-Bass, 1996.

———. "The Limits of Change." *Harvard Education Letter*.

Bibliography for School Restructuring and Reculturing

Fink, D., and Louise Stoll. "Educational Change: Easier Said Than Done." In *International Handbook of Educational Change*. Edited by Andy Hargreaves, et al., 297–321. The Netherlands: Kluwer Academic, 1998.

Fullan, Michael. *Change Forces: Probing the Depths of Educational Reform*. London: Falmer, 1993.

———. *Change Forces: The Sequel*. Bristol, PA: Falmer, 1999.

———. *Change Forces With a Vengeance*. London: RoutledgeFalmer, 2003.

———. *Leading in a Culture of Change*. San Francisco: Jossey-Bass, 2001.

———. "The Meaning of Educational Change: A Quarter of a Century of Learning." In *International Handbook of Educational Change*. Edited by Andy Hargreaves, et al., 214–28. The Netherlands: Kluwer Academic, 1998.

———. *The New Meaning of Educational Change*, 1st ed. New York: Teachers College Press, 1982.

———. *The New Meaning of Educational Change*, 2nd ed. New York: Teachers College Press, 1991.

———. *The New Meaning of Educational Change*, 3rd ed. New York: Teachers College Press, 2001.

———. "The Return of Large-Scale Reform." *The Journal of Educational Change* 1 (2000): 1–23.

———. *What's Worth Fighting for in The Principalship?*, 2nd ed. New York: Teachers College, 1997.

Hargreaves, Andy. *Changing Teachers, Changing Times: Teachers Work and Culture in the Postmodern Age*. New York: Teachers College Press, 1994.

———. *Teaching in the Knowledge Society: Education in the Age of Insecurity*. New York: Teachers College Press, 2003.

———. "Restructuring, Restructuring: Postmodernity and the Prospects for Educational Change." *Journal of Educational Policy* 9 (1993): 47–65.

———. "Cultures of Teaching: A Focus for Change." In *Understanding Teacher Development*. London: Teachers College Press.

———. "Cultures of Teaching and Educational Change." In *The Challenge of School Change: A Collection of Articles*. Arlington Heights, IL: SkyLight, 1997.

———, and Michael Fullan. *What's Worth Fighting for in Your School?*, 2nd ed. New York: Teachers College Press, 1996.

———, and Michael Fullan. *What's Worth Fighting for Out There?* New York: Teachers College Press, 1998.

———, and Ivor Goodson. "Educational Change Over Time? The Sustainability and Non-Sustainability of Three Decades of Secondary School Change and Continuity." In *Educational Change Over Time: Special Issue. Educational Administration Quarterly* 42 (2006): 3–41.

Hopkins, David, et al. *School Improvement in an Era of Change*. New York: Teachers College Press, 1994.

Jacobson, S.L., and James A. Conway. *Educational Leadership in an Age of Reform*. White Plains, NY: Longman, 1990.

Bibliography for School Restructuring and Reculturing

Johnson, Susan M. *Teachers at Work: Achieving Success in Our Schools.* New York: Basic, 1990.

Lieberman, Ann. *Schools As Collaborative Cultures: Creating the Future Now.* New York: Falmer, 1990.

Little, Judith W. "The Persistence of Privacy: Autonomy and Initiative in Teachers' Professional Relations." *Teachers College Record 91* (1990): 509–36.

Lortie, Dan C. *Schoolteacher: A Sociological Study.* Chicago: University of Chicago Press, 2002

Murphy, Joseph. "The Educational Reform Movement of the 1980's: A Comprehensive Analysis." In *The Reform of American Public Education in the 1980's: Perspectives and Cases*, 3–55. Berkeley: McCutchan, 1990.

Murphy, Joseph. *Restructuring Schools: Capturing and Assessing the Phenomena.* New York: Teachers College Press, 1991.

National Commission on Excellence in Education. "A Nation at Risk: The Imperative of Educational Reform."

National Governors Association. *Results in Education.* Washington: NGA, 1989.

Newmann, Fred M., and Associates. *Authentic Achievement: Restructuring Schools for Intellectual Quality.* San Francisco: Jossey-Bass, 1996.

Newmann, F.M., and Gary G. Wehlage, *Successful School Restructuring: A Report to the Public and Educators.* Madison, WI: Wisconsin Center on Education Research, 1995.

Oakes, Jeannie, et al. *Becoming Good American Schools: The Struggle for Civic Virtue in Education Reform.* San Francisco: Jossey-Bass, 2000.

Peterson, Penelope L., et al. "Learning from School Restructuring." *American Educational Research Journal 33* (1996): 119–53.

Purkey, S.D., and Marshall S. Smith. "Effective Schools: A Review." *The Elementary School Journal 83* (1983): 427–52.

Rosenholtz, Susan J. *Teacher's Workplace: The Social Organization of Schools.* New York: Longman, 1989.

Sarason, Seymour B. *The Culture of the School and the Problem of Change.* Boston: Allyn and Bacon, 1971.

———. *The Predictable Failure of Educational Reform: Can We Change Course Before It's Too Late?* San Francisco: Jossey-Bass, 1991.

Schein, Edgar H., et al. *Organizational Culture and Leadership: A Dynamic View.* San Francisco: Jossey-Bass, 1985.

Senge, Peter M. *The Fifth Discipline: The Art and Practice of the Learning Organization.* New York: Currency Doubleday, 1990.

Smith, M.S., and Jennifer A. O'Day. "Systemic School Reform." In *The Politics of Curriculum and Testing: The 1990 Yearbook of the Politics of Education*, 233–67. Philadelphia: Falmer, 1991.

Smylie, M.A., and George S. Perry. "Restructuring Schools for Improving Tomorrow." In *International Handbook of Educational Change.* Edited by

Bibliography for School Restructuring and Reculturing

Andy Hargreaves, et al., 976-1005. The Netherlands: Kluwer Academic, 1998.

Stein, Mary K, et al. "Reform Ideas That Travel Far Afield: The Two Cultures of Reform in New York City's District #2 and San Diego." *Journal of Educational Change* 5 (2000) 161-97.

Stoll, L., and Dean Fink. *Changing Our Schools*. Buckingham: Open University Press, 1996.

Waller, Willard. *The Sociology of Teaching*. New York: J. Wiley & Sons, 1932.

Wehlage, Gary, et al. "Restructuring Urban High Schools: The New Futures Experience." *American Educational Research Journal* 29 (1992): 51-93.

Bibliography for Large Scale Reforms

American Institutes for Research. *An Educators' Guide to School-Wide Reform.* Washington: Author, 1999.
Astuto, Terry A., et al. *Challenges to Dominant Assumptions Controlling Educational Reform.* Andover, MA: Regional Laboratory for the Educational Improvement of the Northeast and Islands, 1993.
Barber, Michael. *High Expectations and Standards.* Unpublished paper. Department for Education and Further Employment, 2001.
———. *Large Scale Reform in England. Paper Presented at Futures of Education Conference.* Universität Zürich Switzerland, 2001.
———. *Accountability vs. Autonomy. Education.* Washington: October 31, 2001.
———, and Judy Sebba. "Reflections on a World-Class Education System." *Cambridge Journal of Education* 29 (1999): 183–93.
Bolman, L.G., and Terrence E. Deal. *Reframing Organizations: Artistry, Choice and Leadership.* San Francisco: Jossey-Bass, 1997.
Berends, Mark. *Facing the Challenges of Whole-School Reform: New American Schools After a Decade.* Santa Monica, CA: RAND, 2002.
———. *Challenges of Conflicting School Reforms: Effects of New American Schools in a High-Poverty District.* Santa Monica, CA: RAND, 2002.
Block, Peter. *Stewardship: Choosing Service Over Self-Interest.* San Francisco: Berrett-Koehler, 1993.
Bryk, Anthony, et al. *Charting Chicago School Reform.* Boulder, CO: Westview, 1998.
Campbell, Elizabeth. "Challenges in Fostering Ethical Knowledge as Professionalism Within Schools As Teaching Communities." *Journal of Educational Change* 6 (2005): 207–26.
Corrie, C., and Andy Hargreaves. "The Sustainability of Innovative Schools As Learning Organizations and Professional Learning Communities during Standardized Reform." In *Educational Change Over Time: Special Issue. Educational Administration Quarterly* 42 (2006): 124–56.
Darling-Hammond, Linda. "The Quiet Revolution: Rethinking Teacher Development." *Educational Leadership* 53 (1996): 4–10.

Bibliography for Large Scale Reforms

Deal, T.E., and Allan A. Kennedy. *Corporate Cultures*. Reading, MA: Addison-Wesley, 1992.

DuFour, Richard. "What Is a Professional Learning Community?" In *On Common Ground: The Power of Professional Learning Communities*, 31–43. Bloomington, IN: Solution Tree, 2005.

———, and Robert Eaker. *Professional Learning Communities at Work: Best Practices for Enhancing Student Achievement*. Blooming, IN: National Educational Service, 1998.

———, et. al. "Recurring Themes of Professional Learning Communities and the Assumptions They Challenge." In *On Common Ground: The Power of Professional Learning Communities*, 7–29. Bloomington, IN: Solution Tree, 2005.

Earl, Lorna. *Large-Scale Education Reform: Life Cycles and Implications for Sustainability*. Reading: Centre for British Teachers, 2003.

Elmore, Richard F. *School Reform from the Inside-Out*. Cambridge: Harvard University Press, 2003.

———, and Deanna Burney. "Investing in Teacher Learning: Staff Development and Instructional Improvement." In L. Darling-Hammond & G. Sykes, eds. *Teaching As the Learning Profession: Handbook of Policy and Practice*, 236–91. San Francisco: Jossey-Bass, 1999.

———. *Building a New Structure for School Leadership*. Washington: Albert Shanker Institute, 2000.

———. *The Hollow Core of Leadership Practice in Education*. Unpublished paper. Harvard University Graduate School of Education, 2004.

———. *School Reform from the Inside Out*. Cambridge: Harvard Education Press, 2004.

Fink, E., and Lauren Resnick. "Developing Principals As Instructional Leaders." *Phi Delta Kappan* 82 (2001): 598–606.

Fullan, Michael. "School Leadership's Unfinished Agenda: Integrating Individual and Organizational Development." *Education Week 27* (2008) :28–36.

———. *Leadership and Sustainability: System Thinkers in Action*. Thousand Oaks, CA: Corwin, 2005.

———. *Leading in a Culture of Change*. San Francisco: Jossey-Bass, 2001.

———, et al. "New Lessons for Districtwide Reform." *Educational Leadership 61* (2004): 42–46.

———. *Change Forces: The Sequel*. Bristol, PA: Falmer, 1999.

———. *Breakthrough*. Thousand Oaks, CA: Corwin Press, 2006.

———. "United Kingdom National Literacy and Numeracy Strategies: Large-scale Reform." *Journal of Educational Change 3* (2002): 1–5.

———, et al. *Implementation of the National Literacy and Numeracy Strategies First Interim Report*. Toronto: OISE, University of Toronto, 1999.

———. "Leadership for the 21st Century: Breaking the Bonds for Dependency." *Educational leadership 55* (1998:) 6–11.

———. *Leading in a Culture of Change*. San Francisco: Jossey-Bass, 2001.

Bibliography for Large Scale Reforms

———. "Leadership Across the System." *Insight* (2004): 14–17.

———. "Professional Learning Communities Writ Large." In *On Common Ground: The Power of Professional Learning Communities*, 209–23. Bloomington, IN: Solution Tree, 2005.

———. *The New Meaning of Educational Change*, 4th ed. New York: Teachers College Press, 2007.

———. *Quality Leadership-Quality Learning: Proof Beyond a Reasonable Doubt*. Toronto: Ontario Institute for Studies in Education, University of Toronto. Paper prepared for the Irish Primary Principals' Network (IPPN), 2006.

———, et al. "Accomplishing Large-Scale Reform: A Tri-level Proposition." In Hernandez, F. and Ivor F. Goodson, eds. *Social Geographies of Educational Change: Drawing a Map for Dissatisfied Travelers*, 1–14. The Netherlands: Kluwer. 2004a.

———. *The New Meaning of Educational Change*. New York: Teachers College Press, 2007.

———. *Turnaround Leadership*. San Francisco: Jossey-Bass, 2006.

———. *The Moral Imperative of School Leadership*. Thousand Oaks, CA: Corwin, 2003.

———. "The Return of Large-Scale Reform." *Journal of Educational Change 1* (2000:) 5–28.

———. "The Three Stories of Education Reform." *Phi Delta Kappan 81* (2000:) 581–84.

———. *What's Worth Fighting for Out There?* New York: Teachers College Press, 1998.

———. *Whole School Reform: Problems and Promises*. Ontario: Ontario Institute for Studies in Education, University of Toronto. Paper commissioned by the Chicago Community Trust, 2001.

Hasser, B.C., and L. Steiner. "Strategies for Scale: Learning from Two Educational Innovations." Cambridge: Occasional paper for The Innovations in American Program at the John F. Kennedy School of Government, Harvard University.

Hargreaves, Andy. "Leading Professional Learning Communities: Moral Choices Amid Murky Realities." In Blankstein, Alan M. *Sustaining Professional Learning Communities*, 1–22. Thousand Oaks, CA: Corwin, 2008.

———. *Teaching in the Knowledge Society: Education in the Age of Insecurity*. New York: Teachers College Press, 2003.

———, and Dean Fink. *Sustainable Leadership*. San Francisco: Wiley, 2006.

———, and Michael Fullan, eds. *Change Wars*. Bloomington: Solution Tree, 2008.

———, and Michael Fullan, *What's Worth Fight for Out There*. New York: Teachers College Press, 1998.

———, et al. *Learning to Change: Beyond Subjects and Standards*. San Francisco: Jossey Bass, 2001.

Bibliography for Large Scale Reforms

———, and Ivor Goodson. "Educational Change Over Time? The Sustainability and Non-Sustainability of Three Decades of Secondary School Change and Continuity." In *Educational Change Over Time: Special Issue. Educational Administration Quarterly* 42 (2006): 3–41.

———. *Teaching in the Knowledge Society: Education in the Age of Insecurity.* New York: Teachers College Press, 2003.

Hord, Shirley M. *Facilitative Leadership: The Imperative for Change.* Austin, TX: Southwest Educational Development Laboratory, 1992.

———. *Professional Learning Communities: Communities of Continuous Inquiry and Improvement.* Austin, TX: Southwest Educational Development Laboratory, 1997.

Huberman, M. "Can Start Teachers Create Learning Communities?" *Educational Leadership* 61 (2004): 52–56.

Huffman, Jane B., et al. *Reculturing Schools As Professional Learning Communities.* Lanham, MD: Scarecrow Education, 2003.

Kruse, Sharon, et al. *Building Professional Community in Schools.* Madison, WI: Center on Organizations and Restructuring of Schools, 1994.

Leithwood, Kenneth A., et al. "A Framework for Research in Large Scale Reform." *Journal of Educational Change* 3 (2002): 7–33.

———, et al. "Large Scale Reform?" Unpublished manuscript, Ontario Institute for Studies in Education, University of Toronto, 1999.

———, et al. "Strategic Leadership for Large Scale Reform: The Case of England's National Literacy and Numeracy Strategy." *School Leadership & Management* 24 (2004): 58–79.

———, et al. *Changing Leadership for Changing Times.* Buckingham: Open University Press, 1999.

———, et al. *How Leadership Influences Student Learning.* New York: Wallace Foundation, 2004.

Levin, B. "Inevitable Tensions in Managing Large Scale Public Service Reform." In *Managing Change in the Public Services,* 136–50. Oxford: Blackwell, 2007.

———. *Reforming Education: From Origins to Outcomes.* London: Routledge Falmer, 2001.

———. "Sustainable, Large Scale Education Renewal." *Journal of Educational Change* 8 (2007:) 323–36.

———, and Michael Fullan. "Learning about System Renewal." *Educational Management, Administration and Leadership* 36 (2008): 289–303.

Louis, K.S., and Sharon D. Kruse. *Professionalism and Community: Perspectives on Reforming Urban School.* Thousand Oaks, CA: Corwin, 1995.

Marzano, Robert, et al. *School Leadership That Works.* Alexandria, VA: Association for Supervision and Curriculum Development, 2005.

McLaughlin, M., and Joan Talbert. *Professional Communities and The Work of High School Teaching.* Chicago: University of Chicago Press, 2001.

Bibliography for Large Scale Reforms

———, and Joan Talbert. *Contexts That Matter for Teaching and Learning*. Stanford: Center for Research on the Context of Secondary School Teaching, Stanford University, 1993.

———, and Dana Mitra. "Theory-Based Change and Change-Based Theory: Going Deeper, Going Broader. *Journal of Educational Change* 2 (2001): 301–23.

———, and Joan Talbert. *Building School-Based Teacher Learning Communities*. New York: Teachers College Press, 2006.

McNeil, Linda. *Contradictions of School Reform*. London: Routledge, 2000.

Méndez-Morse, Sylvia. "Leadership Characteristics That Facilitate School Change." Austin, TX: Southwest Educational Development Laboratory.

Newmann, Fred M., et al. "Professional Development That Addressed School Capacity." Paper presented at the annual meeting of the American Educational Research Association. New Orleans, LA, 2000.

———, and Gary Wehlage, G. *Successful School Restructuring*. Madison, WI: Center on Organization and Restructuring of Schools, 1995.

Resnick, L., and Thomas K. Glennan. "Leadership for Learning: A Theory of Action for Urban School Districts." In *School Districts and Instructional Renewal*, 165–72. New York: Teachers College Press, 2002.

Rosenholtz, Susan J. *Teacher's Workplace: The Social Organization of Schools*. New York: Longman, 1989.

Scribner, Jay P., et al. "Creating Professional Communities in Schools throughOrganizational Learning: An Evaluation of a School Improvement Process." *Educational Administration Quarterly* 35 (1999): 130–60.

Senge, Peter M. *The Fifth Discipline: The Art and Practice of the Learning Organization*. New York: Currency Doubleday, 1990.

———. *Leading Learning Organizations: The Bold, The Powerful and The Visible*. Cambridge: MIT Center for Organizational Learning, 1996.

Sergiovanni, Thomas. *Leadership: What's in It For Schools?* New York: Routledge Falmer, 2002.

———. *The Lifeworld of Leadership*. San Francisco: Jossey-Bass, 2000.

Slavin, Robert E., et al. *Success for All: A Relentless Approach to Prevention and Early Intervention in Elementary Schools*. Arlington, VA: Educational Research Service, 1992.

———, and Nancy A. Madden. *Disseminating Success for All*. Baltimore, MD: The John Hopkins University, 1998.

Smith, M.S., and Jennifer A. O'Day. "Systemic School Reform." In *The Politics of Curriculum and Testing: The 1990 Yearbook of the Politics of Education*, 233–67. Philadelphia: Falmer, 1991.

Stein, Mary K., et al. "Reform Ideas That Travel Far Afield: The Two Cultures of Reform in New York City's District #2 and San Diego." *Journal of Educational Change* 5 (2000): 161–97.

Stoll, Louise, et al. *Professional Learning Communities: Source Materials for School Leaders and Other Leaders of Professional Learning*. Nottingham: National College for School Leadership, 2006.

Bibliography for Large Scale Reforms

Spillane, James P., et al. "Investigating School Leadership Practice: A Distributive Perspective." *Educational Researcher* 30 (2001): 23–28.

Taylor, Rosemary T. "Shaping the Culture of Learning Communities." *Principal Leadership* 3 (2002): 42–45.

Waters, Tim, et al. *Balanced Leadership: What 30 Years of Research Tell Us About the Effects of Leadership on Student Achievement.* Denver, CO: Mid-Continent Research for Education and Learning, 2003.

Wenger, E. *Communities of Practice.* Cambridge: Cambridge University Press, 1998.

Whyte, David. *The Heart Aroused: Poetry and The Preservation of the Soul in Corporate America.* New York: Currency Doubleday, 1994.

www.ingramcontent.com/pod-product-compliance
Lightning Source LLC
Chambersburg PA
CBHW070509090426
42735CB00012B/2708